Widening Participation, Higher Education and Non-Traditional Students

Catherine A. Marshall • Sam J. Nolan • Douglas P. Newton
Editors

Widening Participation, Higher Education and Non-Traditional Students

Supporting Transitions through Foundation Programmes

palgrave
macmillan

Editors
Catherine A. Marshall
Durham University
Durham, United Kingdom

Douglas P. Newton
Durham University
Durham, United Kingdom

Sam J. Nolan
Durham University
Durham, United Kingdom

ISBN 978-1-349-94968-7   ISBN 978-1-349-94969-4   (eBook)
DOI 10.1057/978-1-349-94969-4

Library of Congress Control Number: 2016940531

© The Editor(s) (if applicable) and The Author(s) 2016
The author(s) has/have asserted their right(s) to be identified as the author(s) of this work in accordance with the Copyright, Designs and Patents Act 1988.
This work is subject to copyright. All rights are solely and exclusively licensed by the Publisher, whether the whole or part of the material is concerned, specifically the rights of translation, reprinting, reuse of illustrations, recitation, broadcasting, reproduction on microfilms or in any other physical way, and transmission or information storage and retrieval, electronic adaptation, computer software, or by similar or dissimilar methodology now known or hereafter developed.
The use of general descriptive names, registered names, trademarks, service marks, etc. in this publication does not imply, even in the absence of a specific statement, that such names are exempt from the relevant protective laws and regulations and therefore free for general use.
The publisher, the authors and the editors are safe to assume that the advice and information in this book are believed to be true and accurate at the date of publication. Neither the publisher nor the authors or the editors give a warranty, express or implied, with respect to the material contained herein or for any errors or omissions that may have been made.

Cover illustration: © redtea / Getty

Printed on acid-free paper

This Palgrave imprint is published by Springer Nature
The registered company is Macmillan Publishers Ltd. London

Foreword

The global landscape of higher education provision is changing rapidly. Many UK universities have pursued an active internationalisation agenda while at the same time seeking to ensure fair access for under-represented groups of students. One innovative approach has been to develop an in-house foundation centre aimed at UK mature students and younger international students. This book explores the rationale behind this approach and how it fits into the landscape of national foundation year provision. The chapters describe various innovative approaches to admissions, marketing and recruitment and to the development and delivery of curricula which support students hoping to study further in a research-intensive university. The book concludes with three case studies of students who have gone on to successful careers within and outside academia.

The contributors to the book were praised for supporting good practice in the field of widening participation and social mobility in the 2012 Milburn report *University Challenge: How Higher Education Can Advance Social Mobility*. The lessons learned from this approach will interest all who work to widen access to higher education.

Professor Stuart Corbridge
Vice Chancellor and Warden
Durham University, UK

Preface

Obstacles, real and imagined, stand between some people and higher education. Some may have left school early and/or lack the expected paper qualifications, some may have had family obligations which had priority, others may see a disability or the kind of life they live as denying them access, while others see higher education as something "people like us just do not do." The need to include people like this, to *widen participation* in higher education, has received a lot of attention. It is variously seen as having the potential to support the national economy, to alter the nature of society, to enable equal opportunity, and to reduce alienation stemming from perceived or real exclusion.

From time to time, various strategies have been devised to encourage wider participation, and higher education institutions may be offered incentives if they increase their intake of under-represented groups, or are subject to disadvantages if they do not. But much less is available on the practicalities of making these students' experience of higher education a successful one. This has been a personal and collective interest of the contributors to this book. Bringing together the various strands of interest has allowed us to describe the endeavour, and how the students' needs may be met as they follow an introductory, *foundation year*, a preliminary year, or Year 0, in a university, preparing them to begin an undergraduate degree. During this year, students' knowledge and skills are refreshed, updated, and extended, and they are inducted into ways of learning that are very different from those they met in school.

In what follows, we sometimes refer to these foundation year students as "non-traditional" students. They comprise those who are subject to obstacles like those mentioned earlier, and they generally would find direct entry on a degree course of their choice unlikely, fruitless, or too daunting. Many could be described as "mature" students, largely from the UK, who are older than the majority of undergraduates commonly found in the UK's higher education institutions; that is to say, they are over 21 years old, and often much older, often having had paid employment in the intervening years between school and the foundation year. Such students may feel there is or has been more than one obstacle between them and higher education. Others, described here as "international," are from all parts of the world, particularly the Far East, and tend to be younger and lack the paper qualifications required for direct entry to a particular degree course. The term "non-traditional student" is a wide and somewhat vague one and can vary with context and cohort. We have indicated what it commonly means for us, but readers will be able to relate and interpret our accounts to suit their own contexts and their own students and, hopefully, find them of some practical use.

CAM, SJN, DPN,
Durham University, 2016

Acknowledgements

The editors and contributors thank Rachel Dunn for her work in reading and painstakingly putting these diverse chapters into a uniform layout, and drawing our attention to some errors of commission and omission. Any that still remain are ours.

All editors and contributors are currently based at Durham University, except Sarah Learmonth, who is at Cambridge University.

Contents

1. **Barriers to Accessing Higher Education**   1
   Catherine A. Marshall

2. **Understanding Foundation Year Provision**   19
   Steve Leech, Catherine A. Marshall, and Geoff Wren

3. **Language Issues Facing Non-Traditional Students: Some Problems and Solutions**   41
   Megan Bruce, Simon Rees, and Julie Wilson

4. **Teaching Mathematics to Adults: Integrating New and Old Knowledge**   57
   Mary Dodd, Jean Mathias, and Sam J. Nolan

5. **Breaking Barriers: Overcoming Anxieties in Practical Science**   73
   Sam J. Nolan, Simon Rees, and Carole Rushall

6. **Selecting Mature Learners: A Toolkit for Admissions Tutors**   89
   Ian Moreton

7 Challenges and Opportunities in Using Facebook to Build a Community for Students at a UK University   105
   Nick Pearce and Sarah Learmonth

8 Engendering an Online Community: Supporting Students on the Transition into University Life   119
   Sam J. Nolan, Megan Bruce, and Steve Leech

9 Culture Shock: Applying the Lessons from International Student Acculturation to Non-Traditional Students   133
   Catherine A. Marshall and Jinhua Mathias

10 Adjusting Teaching Practices for Mature Adults to Incorporate Understandings of Affective Processes and Self-efficacy in Maths   151
   Mary D. Dodd

11 Students' Academic Emotions, Their Effects and Some Suggestions for Teaching Practices   165
   Douglas P. Newton

12 Stories with a Foundation   179
   Catherine A. Marshall

Index   189

Contributors

Megan Bruce, BA (Dunelm), MA, DELTA, SFHEA is a senior teaching fellow and Director of Learning and Teaching in the Foundation Centre. Her disciplinary background is Linguistics and Lexicography, and her scholarly interests include corpus building and native-speaker English for Academic Purposes (EAP).

Mary Dodd, Ed.D, M.A, BSc, ACGI, FHEA, PGCE is a senior teaching fellow at Durham University. Following her first degree in Chemical Engineering, Mary taught a variety of maths and science courses before joining the Foundation Centre in 1995. Mary's scholarly interests focus mainly on adults' mathematics learning and the interaction of previous learning and emotion with new mathematics learning.

Sarah Learmonth, BA is a criminology postgraduate student at the University of Cambridge. Sarah is a previous student of the Durham University Foundation Centre, where she later held the role of Social Media Assistant. Following completion of her undergraduate degree at Durham University, Sarah is now researching technology within prison education programmes.

Steve Leech, BSc, MSc, FHEA is a teaching fellow with a disciplinary background in Anthropology and has taught at the Foundation Centre for 11 years. Steve's scholarly interests include fair access in recruitment, widening participation, and supporting care leavers and veterans in higher education. Steve is the Secretary of the Foundation Year Network, a national body which represents foundation year practitioners in the UK.

Catherine A. Marshall, MA (Oxon), EdD, PGCE(Science) is Director of the Foundation Centre at Durham University and Chair of the national Foundation Year Network. Catherine joined the Foundation Centre in 1994 and has been instrumental in its development. Her scholarly interests focus on students' self-efficacy and conscientiousness and how these affect student outcomes.

Jinhua Mathias, PhD, FHEA is a teaching fellow with a disciplinary background in Mathematics and Engineering and has taught at the Durham University's Foundation Centre for some six years. Jinhua's scholarly interests include international student resilience and cultural adjustment, peer mentoring and mature students learning of mathematics.

Ian Moreton, FRSA is a teaching fellow with a background in engineering and has taught at Durham University's Foundation Centre for some eight years. Ian's scholarly interests focus on issues surrounding the selection of students in a WP context.

Douglas P. Newton, BSc, MEd, PhD, DSc, SFHEA is a professor with a background in science and is a lecturer in Science and Technology Education. His scholarly interests include strategies to support productive purposeful thinking, such as reasoning, understanding, creative and critical thinking, and wisdom. Some recent, related books are *Teaching for Understanding* and *Thinking with Feeling* (Routledge, London).

Sam J. Nolan, MSci, PhD, SFHEA is Assistant Director of the Centre for Academic, Researcher and Organisation Development at Durham University. From 2010 to 2015 Sam led the Foundation Centre's Scholarship Forum and co-developed the Centre's strategy for Scholarship of Teaching and Learning. Sam's own scholarly interests include student transition, laboratory skills development, and conceptual understanding.

Nick Pearce, PhD teaches sociology and anthropology at the Durham University Foundation Centre, and managed their social media presences across Facebook, Twitter and Instagram. He has published widely around the use of social media such as YouTube and Pinterest in his teaching and was recently named in the top 50 UK higher education social media influencers by JISC.

Simon Rees, BSc, PhD, SFHEA is a teaching fellow with a disciplinary background in Chemistry and has taught at the Foundation Centre for some six years. Simon's scholarly interests include the language of chemistry and virtual experimentation.

Carole Rushall, BSc, MSc, FHEA is a teaching fellow with a background in Environmental Science, Geology and Cartography and has taught at the Foundation Centre for 16 years. Carole's scholarly interests include developing virtual fieldwork resources and mature student transition into higher education.

Julie Wilson, BA is a teaching fellow who has been teaching at the Foundation Centre for six years. Her disciplinary background is in English and linguistics, which prompted her current interest in the new alternative means of providing feedback, and student motivation and resilience.

Geoff Wren, BA MA CELTA is a teaching fellow with a subject background in the Human Sciences (particularly Anthropology and Sociology) and Education. He has been with the Foundation Centre for 15 years. Geoff's scholarly interests include inequalities in education and lack of fair access.

List of Figures

Fig. 5.1	Example of a screenshot from Chemistry ISE	77
Fig. 5.2	Example of a screenshot from a Physics AR	79
Fig. 5.3	Example of a screenshot from Chemistry AR	80
Fig. 5.4	Example of a screenshot from virtual field trip	81
Fig. 7.1	Total likes on Facebook during project lifetime	110
Fig. 7.2	Demographic data	111
Fig. 7.3	Year of entry	113
Fig. 7.4	Categories of fans	114
Fig. 8.1	Visits by registered users of the site during summer 2012 (*top*) and 2013 (*bottom*). Weekly peaks can be seen during September as students either watch live or engage with the transmission of each weekly webchat	127
Fig. 8.2	Integrated visits of registered users to the website during the summers of 2012–2014 by country of users. This indicates significant use by both home mature students and younger international students	128
Fig. 10.1	Comparison of anxiety about maths study with anxiety about foundation study in general	153
Fig. 10.2	A scattergram to compare scores with maths anxiety rating	154
Fig. 11.1	A model of students' dual system for maintaining their well-being: events are noticed, judged for bearing upon goals, beliefs and values, and result in responses according to the judgements	166
Fig. 11.2	The development of anxieties before, during and after a high-stake test	173

List of Tables

Table 2.1	Foundation year provision by university group	29
Table 2.2	Availability of foundation year by academic discipline	30
Table 2.3	Use of foundation programmes by universities by ranking	35
Table 2.4	Matrix of modelled delivery combinations	37
Table 5.1	Summary of how each class of learning objects addresses the stages of the model	82
Table 5.2	Summary of how each class of learning objects addresses the conversational framework of Laurillard	86
Table 8.1	Summarised from (Keenan, 2012) on the aim and mechanism of online pre-arrival support at several UK HEIs	123

CHAPTER 1

Barriers to Accessing Higher Education

Catherine A. Marshall

CAPITAL, HABITUS AND FIELD

Bourdieu's work explored the interaction between three concepts—capital, habitus and field—which he used to explain the maintenance of a stratified society. He expanded the notion of capital, arguing that it was not just tangible economic capital which could be used to account for the structure of society in terms of which individuals or groups held power and status, but that so could other forms of capital, which he referred to as cultural capital and social capital (1986). He used the term cultural capital to refer to those social assets which support social mobility beyond economic means including aspects such as style of speech, dress, ownership of books or pictures, or knowledge of types of music and art forms; his term social capital referred to the social networks and connections within a group of people. His view was that there was misrecognition of the value of different forms of culture as being something intrinsic to that form (e.g. piece of music, artwork or literature), whereas in fact it is arbitrary and defined by the dominant group. He proposed that in the education system it is those aspects of culture deemed worthy by the dominant group which are

C.A. Marshall (✉)
Foundation Centre, University of Durham, Pelaw House, Leazes Road, Durham DH1 1TA, UK

© The Editor(s) (if applicable) and The Author(s) 2016
C.A. Marshall et al. (eds.), *Widening Participation, Higher Education and Non-Traditional Students*,
DOI 10.1057/978-1-349-94969-4_1

valued and studied (1976). This consequently means that individuals from the dominant group will have an advantage in education as their familial background will have allowed them to develop a habitus which values and leads to the acquisition of the cultural capital required to do well in education (Moore, 2004). Bourdieu's theory was that the different forms of capital were convertible; for example, cultural capital can be converted to educational qualifications leading to greater economic capital, and in the same way that children can inherit their wealth from their parents, so too can cultural and social capital be transmitted within the family (1986). In this way, those groups with the cultural resources, particularly with regard to education, use them to maintain their status (Swartz, 1997).

The concept of habitus was developed by Bourdieu to describe a "system of shared social dispositions and cognitive structures which generates perceptions, appreciations and actions" (1984, p. 279). These are the dispositions inculcated in an individual by the environment and culture in which one grows up, which Bourdieu describes as unconscious internalisation of the chances of success of an individual from a particular class. The habitus produces certain actions and attitudes within particular fields, with Bourdieu describing fields as structured spaces with varying degrees of autonomy which produce their own values and behavioural constraints that are relatively independent from other fields (Naidoo, 2004). Bourdieu uses the term "field" to describe the setting in which the interactions of capital are sited; the arena where the social relationships are structured in terms of power. An individual's role in a particular field is determined by the cultural capital one holds in that field and how well one's habitus is adapted to it (Bourdieu, 1993).

It has been argued (e.g. Archer, 1970; Jenkins, 1992) that Bourdieu's ideas are particular to French society However, Robbins (2004) argues that his ideas are transcultural and transferable and that there has been a failure to engage with Bourdieu's ideas in the UK. This chapter considers the effect of capital and habitus of individuals in the fields of formal education in the UK.

Which Groups Are Under-represented?

The generally accepted consensus is that non-traditional students in HE include "women, ethnic minorities, mature and working class students and students with disabilities" providing one side of a dichotomy with "a privileged minority of young, white, Western men without disabilities or without the constraints of employment or dependents" on the other (Hinton-Smith, 2012, p. 4). Although Bourdieu's work focused on the dominant and dominated groups in terms of social class, it has been argued that it is also applicable to gender, racial and ethnic disadvantage (McClelland, 1990, p. 105; Reay, 2004) and Dillabough contends that Bourdieu's work is key to understanding "the problems of subordination, differentiation and hierarchy, and to expose the possibilities, as well as the limits, of gendered self-hood" (2004, p. 503). Reay considers that the inclusion of race and gender differences when studying habitus is particularly of importance when exploring smaller research contexts (2004).

A very important distinction to make is that individuals frequently fall into two or more of these categories making it difficult to disaggregate whether a disadvantage is due to sex, class, gender or ethnicity and Egerton (2000) noted that disadvantaged students are more likely to come to HE as mature students.

Students from Lower Socioeconomic Backgrounds

Although there is evidence that participation in HE has been improving for people from lower socioeconomic groups, there is still a great deal of disparity and the pattern of participation which demonstrates uneven distribution across types of Higher Education Institutions (HEIs). Yorke (2012) compared the proportions of young people from lower socioeconomic groups in old and new universities and found that on average, new universities had 37.7% of their young people from the National Statistics Socio-Economic Classification (NS-SEC) categories 4, 5, 6 and 7 compared to 22% for old universities. He also compared the increase in participation in the 12 years between 1994 and 2006 and found that for students from advantaged backgrounds the increase was from 50% to 55%, while for those from disadvantaged backgrounds the increase was from 13% to 16%.

Ethnic Minorities

The increase in upward social mobility for ethnic groups in Britain has been observed since the 1960s with education seen as a major driver (Shiner & Modood, 2002). The efforts of economic migrants to better themselves and their identification of education with improved social mobility is one of the explanations given for the over-representation of ethnic minority students in HE, nearly twice the proportion of university entrants compared with the general population of ethnic minority 18–24 year olds (Shiner & Modood, 2002). However, the pattern of participation for minority ethnic groups is not evenly distributed across HEIs, with a greater proportion found in new universities and, as a consequence, producing under-representation in elite universities (Shiner & Modood, 2002).

Female Students

At the beginning of the expansion of HE in the 1960s, women were in the minority compared with men (Tight, 2012). Five decades on, the situation has reversed and now commentators are beginning to discuss men as the under-represented group (Gorard, 2008). However, the picture is more complex as there is uneven participation by men and women in elite universities, with women being less well represented (Tight, 2012).

Mature Students

Studies of adult learners have demonstrated that there are personal, social and economic benefits when adults return to learning (Knightley, 2006). Much of the focus of this work has been on raising the aspirations of the learners rather than changing the cultures inherent in the educational establishments (Tett, 2004). Yet, there is evidence that HE may benefit from mature student participation.

A study to explore retention in HE (e.g. David, 2012) showed that while students from lower socioeconomic backgrounds were less likely to be retained than more traditional students, this difference was less marked in mature students. This may be because they are making up for their lack of cultural capital with other skills and qualities, such as, time management skills.

How Unfair Is this Representation?

Gorard (2008) contends that the unfair under-representation of particular groups in HE has yet to be established, pointing out that the demographic landscape in the UK has changed considerably in the post-War years making it difficult to make comparisons across time. There are difficulties in defining and measuring social class as well as defining and measuring participation in HE. Gorard (2008) argues that as 92% of the population as a whole is White, based on the 2001 census, while they make up only 84% of undergraduate (UG) population, that it is actually the White proportion of the population who are under-represented. He also notes that the increased participation by women in HE has led to an under-representation of men across all categories. Given the data available to him, Gorard notes that the odds ratio of enrolling in a degree between the higher three social groups and the lower three social groups fell from 7.9 in 1990 to 4.4 in 1999 indicating that social class participation in HE is improving. The inequality is still apparent; data from the 2001 census showed that 50% of those aged 18–19 in the higher three social groups were accepted to degree courses compared with 19% of the lower three social groups.

Tight (2012) reaches the same conclusions as Gorard in that the picture for women and ethnic minorities does not indicate under-representation. However, he does qualify this with some concerns about women's under-representation in certain institutions and the fact that ethnic minorities, like women, are over-represented, but they are concentrated in the new universities maintaining a level of inequality of opportunity; that professions providing wealth and status are more likely to recruit from the elite universities (Milburn, 2009). Likewise, although there have been some advances for mature students, they too tend to be concentrated in new universities, and as part-time students, struggle to achieve parity in terms of funding (Tight, 2012). Tight acknowledges Gorard's point that it is prior academic achievement which provides the barrier for students from lower socioeconomic groups to access university; however, there is evidence that, while there is correlation between A-level (Advanced General Certificate of Education) scores and achievement in HE, this correlation is less marked for young people from disadvantaged backgrounds (Milburn, 2012).

Reasons for Under-representation

Cultural Capital and Inadequate Compulsory Education

All children in the UK are required by law to receive education up to the age of 16, but the question is whether all children receive an adequate education to enable them to continue their education beyond that. In a paper outlining the different forms of capital, Bourdieu described how his notion of cultural capital arose as a theory "to explain the unequal scholastic achievement of children originating from the different social classes by relating academic success… to the distribution of cultural capital between the classes" (1986) and he has written extensively on the issue of how the cultural differences between social classes is maintained in the education system, causing inequity in educational experience and reproduction of the class system (Bourdieu & Passeron, 1990).

Bourdieu argues that the cultural capital given to middle class children enables them to access the education offered by the system and that schools do not promote and reward natural ability, but social ability. Children of lower social classes must acquire, through education, certain knowledge, language and ways of behaving, which children of higher social class receive as a matter of course through their up-bringing. This is enforced by parental attitude, peer groups and teachers. Consequently, a child of lower social class must do far better than one of higher class to reap the same rewards (Bourdieu, 1976); "Parents pass on their cultural heritage to their children…" (Swartz, 1997, p. 198).

The A-Level System Favours the Middle Class

Bourdieu was critical of the way that the national examination system in France presented advantages to those students who had greater levels of cultural capital, arguing that examinations "tend to measure ability in linguistic expression as much as mastery of subject matter" (Swartz, 1997, p. 200). He argued that examinations give the impression of being meritocratic while they actually favour the culturally privileged.

Bourdieu's concerns about examinations favouring students who come from higher classes may have relevance in the UK, where General Certificate of Secondary Education (GCSEs) and then A levels are used as the main basis for measuring potential to do well at university. There is evidence that achievement in these examinations is unequally distributed across different classes of students. According to Universities UK (2009), only a third of the children eligible for free school meals (FSM)—used as a measure of socioeconomic deprivation—achieve five A–C grade GCSEs at the age of 16 compared with two-thirds of other children. This disparity continues to be observed at the age of 19, with 32% of FSM children attaining a level 3 qualification compared with 57% of other children. In 2011, only 4% of FSM children achieved three grade As at A level which was less than half the rate of the rest of young people who attended state schools (Milburn, 2012). At the other end of the scale, 11% of A-level students who are privately educated account for 32% of those who achieve at least three grade As at A level and 39% achieving three A star grades (Milburn, 2012).

RECRUITMENT LEADING TO REPRODUCTION OF SOCIETY

Selection Based on Cultural Capital in France

Bourdieu considered ways in which the education system reproduced society's structure in terms of how students were selected for university; he explored the examination system, the notion of facilitating subjects, the importance of language, and discrepancies in the types of HEIs attended by different groups of students. He observed that, in France the general curriculum required for elite HEIs was dominated by humanist studies, which were less likely to be studied by students from a disadvantaged background; such students were more likely to study technical or vocational subjects which would provide them with skills that were required by the job market. He also made the point that possession of cultural capital would provide an advantage to students studying humanist subjects, both in terms of content matter and having the language skills to express themselves in an academically acceptable format. Bourdieu argued that these differences led to elite institutions selecting those students with advantages of cultural capital, whereas disadvantaged students received their higher education from less prestigious institutions. He made the observation that this then had an impact later in life noting that "the type and prestige of educational institution attended are as influential for later careers as are the number of years spent in schooling" (Swartz, 1997, p. 193).

Selection in the UK

There have been studies conducted to explore whether these effects can be seen in the current UK HE system and the focus has been to consider A-level qualifications of applicants and the type of school attended. It has been suggested that UK HEIs and the UK government are ambivalent about non-traditional students, valuing their status as subjects of research, but then tolerating them rather than prizing them (Woodley & Wilson, 2002) and that they prefer to focus recruitment activities on the easiest students—high-scoring A-level students—who need the least support to achieve a good university standard (Watson, 2007). There is evidence that even when students from state schools do achieve the A levels required for elite universities, they are still under-represented. The Sutton Trust (2004) refers to a missing 3,000 state school students who achieve the grades required for the top universities in the UK, but do not gain a place, concluding that the university admissions process acts in favour of privately educated school students. A further problem with the process of using A levels as the measure of potential is that evidence indicates that students from state schools perform better in final degree outcome than privately educated students with the same grades. There appears to be an effect of teaching in the private sector which enhances students' performance at A level, but which does not persist through university (Hoare & Johnston, 2011; Ogg, Zimdars, & Heath, 2009).

An example of the discrepancy between a private education and a state education is the different educational capital in terms of the subjects taken in the two types of schools. The Russell Group of universities (2011) states that there are "facilitating subjects" which are likely to be a requirement for entry to selective universities; specifically, Maths, individual sciences, English, other languages and History. Students studying their A levels at comprehensive schools are less likely to study these subjects; for example, in 2011, only 40% of students studying at comprehensive schools took one or more of the individual sciences compared with 63% of those at private schools (Milburn, 2012). This means that state school students are more likely to be disadvantaged when applying to university, as they will not have studied the subjects that are required to gain entry.

Admissions Bias in Elite Universities

In an analysis of University and Colleges Admissions Services (UCAS) data, Boliver (2013) investigated the degree to which this under-representation was a result of choices by the candidates, or decisions by the universities. Her results showed that those from lower social class backgrounds were less likely to apply to Russell Group universities, and that those from Black, Pakistani or Bangladeshi backgrounds were likely to apply, but less likely to be offered a place and those from state schools were both less likely to apply and less likely to be offered a place once they had applied. This was not based on inequalities in prior achievement; she found applicants from state schools applying to Russell Group universities were on average better qualified in terms of their A-level grades than those from private schools and they also needed to be better qualified to gain an offer (Boliver, 2013). Obviously, the reasons behind these differences are likely to be complex. For example, qualitative research (Archer, 2007; Archer & Hutchings, 2000; Archer, Hutchings, & Ross, 2003) indicates that the types of universities typified by the Russell Group are likely to be perceived as the "preserve of the privately educated White upper-middle class" (Boliver, 2013, p. 347) which may put off Black and Minority Ethnic (BME) students or students from lower classes from applying. Boliver also makes the point that one reason for the disparity may be the differential between predicted grades for students at independent schools and others. The work of Bourdieu would suggest that the content and language employed by applicants in the personal statements of their UCAS application forms may also lead to variations in selection of students from less culturally advantaged backgrounds. This was the contention of the Sutton Trust in their report of a summary of research into UCAS personal statements (Jones, 2013). They demonstrated that in three main areas likely to be affected by cultural and social capital, that is, fluency of expression, work-related activity and extra-curricular activity, there were large discrepancies between students from state and independent schools.

Students from working class backgrounds often lack the support at home to enable them to negotiate a pathway through education. The students in a study by Bowl (2003) repeatedly describe missed opportunities due to lack of knowledge or understanding of choices. Bowl argues that teachers and schools have greater control over the choices of working class students than their middle class peers because of the informational disadvantages of the parents of such children. This lack of information continues through to the HE experience meaning that students have little information about what to expect or how to access support.

The Effect of Habitus: Alienation of Alternative Learner Identities

In the previous section, there was evidence that some of the underrepresentation of students from certain groups may be due to the fact that they just do not apply to certain elite institutions and this relates to one of the key themes running through Bourdieu's work on the education system which emphasises the role of self-selection by the student in academic choices. Choice of institution, choice of course, retention or withdrawal and, in fact, whether to apply to university or not is shaped by an individual's expectations of whether someone from their social background is likely to succeed academically or not. This self-selection can be explained by Bourdieu's concept of habitus which he describes as the "totality of learned habits, bodily skills, styles, tastes and other non-discursive knowledges that might be said to 'go without saying' for a specific group" (1990, pp. 66–67). Bourdieu considered these ideas to be largely unconscious rather than rational and a permanent aspect of an individual (Swartz, 1997).

The Effect of Habitus on Attitudes Towards Education

In *Reproduction in Education, Society and Culture* Bourdieu and Passeron describe the concept of habitus as a way of perceiving, analysing and acting on the world around us. They describe the pedagogic practices of the family as being greatly influential on the formation of an individual's habitus (Bourdieu & Passeron, 1990). Berger and Luckmann make a similar proposal that the social identity that a child develops is dependent on the filtering of their social world by those around them (1966). The significant others (usually close family members) to the child determine how the children place themselves in the world. "Thus the lower-class child not only absorbs a lower-class perspective on the social world, he absorbs it in the idiosyncratic coloration given it by his parents" (1966, p. 151). This socialisation process is highly dependent not only on cognitive learning, but also on the emotional attachment that the children have towards their significant others. This highly charged emotional element leads to a level of resistance to challenges to this primary socialisation.

The Effect of Fees and Finance

Ultimately students may be making the choice not to attend university because the financial implications provide too much of a barrier and there is speculation that, not only do students from lower socioeconomic groups choose not to go to university because of a fear of debt, but that the new fees regime introduced in 2012 will further reduce participation by disadvantaged students (Callender & Jackson, 2005); "Inequality thus remains self-perpetuating to some extent; it is harder to escape poverty having grown up in it" (Hinton-Smith, 2012, p. 5). There is also a regional imbalance in HE participation which may be exacerbated by the regional variation in debt aversion (Bachan, 2013). There are large differences between the participation rates of English regions, for example, young people living in London are 50% more likely to enter HE than those in the North-East of England. Given that the government estimates that a graduate earns around £100,000 additional net income over a lifetime compared with a non-graduate, it is likely that economic disparities between regions are going to grow, maintaining the regional disparities in respect of the financial barriers to HE (PAC, 2009).

The pattern of recruitment of mature students has been similar to that observed with the participation of lower socioeconomic groups, that the introduction of fees has seen a decline in applications by 15–20% (Milburn, 2012). There is recognition that WP groups and especially adult learners are the most likely to experience financial concerns as a significant barrier (Pollard, 2008). Such groups are often geographically grounded, due to family and financial responsibilities (Pollard, 2008) and therefore less able to relocate in order to access institutions with lower course fees.

The recent global recession has deepened cuts to education, and with UK HEIs expecting 80% spending cuts, the majority introduced fees at or near the £9,000 maximum in the academic year 2012–13 (Higher Education Funding Council for England, 2010). The effect of fees at the previous level of around £3000 has been noted in increased rates of applications to the Open University from traditional-age students, increase in applications to international universities and evidence of students waiting until 21 before commencing university so that they are assessed on their own financial income rather than their parents' (Hinton-Smith, 2012). The increase of fees to £9,000 is likely to produce more changes in student behaviour. Over the last few years, demand has outstripped supply for HE places, and perhaps the increase in fees will redress the balance by deterring poorer students.

There have been further financial cuts which may affect students from disadvantaged backgrounds. *Aim higher*, a national programme to widen participation to HE in England, was disbanded in July 2011 and its replacement by the National Scholarship Programme does not provide financial support for outreach work; universities are expected to fund their own outreach work from the £9,000 fees and any student support is for the first year only (Higher Education Funding Council for England, 2010). The Educational Maintenance Allowance (EMA) provided support for 16–18 education for students from disadvantaged backgrounds—predominantly Black and Minority Ethnic and single parent families–and was credited with being an important factor in increasing social mobility (Milburn, 2012). There was evidence that it improved retention and achievement at 16–18 with 30% of students indicating that without the EMA they would have left education. The EMA has been removed in England since 2010. The evidence on bursaries and fee waivers for university students is more mixed, however, and does not seem to show any change in behaviour of student choice (Corver, 2010). Perhaps the mechanism is subtler and related to self-efficacy beliefs; the message may be that selective universities do not have students from lower socio-economic backgrounds because they are not welcome and the introduction of higher fees is reinforcing the message that this is not a place where disadvantaged students are welcome.

Under-representation Has a Complex Mix of Reasons

While it is interesting to consider the relative merits of the three outlined factors which may be responsible for under-representation—poor initial education, recruitment practices or alienation from the dominant culture—it is likely that the real picture will be a complex mix of all of them in addition to other factors. Bourdieu recognised that there were other factors involved in the representation of different groups in education pointing out that "elimination or survival in the system are not randomly distributed amongst individuals of the same class, but are themselves liable to be linked to social or cultural criteria differentiating sub-groups within a class" (Bourdieu & Passeron, 1990, p. 104).

In order to explore this mix of factors affecting engagement in HE, Gorard and Selwyn (2005) conducted a set of interviews with adults in the UK which described their lifelong learning participation and investigated the patterns of behaviour with regard to engagement with post-compulsory education. What was interesting about this study was that it involved home-based interviews in four different electoral wards in England and Wales using systematic sampling to be representative of economic activity, education attainment levels, age and sex, rather than data collected from individuals already engaged in lifelong learning. Consequently, the data can be used to consider the factors which affect non-participation in post-compulsory education. Although the study reports data collected on 1000 respondents, they claim to have collated similar evidence from 10,000 adults. The outcome showed that the "key social determinants predicting lifelong participation in learning are time, place, sex, family and initial schooling" (Gorard & Selwyn, 2005, p. 1211).

There seem to be cultural attitudes to an individual's identity as a learner which are affected by the era in which they grew up, their local environment while growing up, for example, how economically advantaged the area was, their initial experience of schooling, how successful it was, and most strongly their parents' social class and educational experience. These factors are likely to affect how relevant an individual considers continuing education to their own situation. For example, if there are very few occupational opportunities why would an individual use resources to train for non-existent jobs; if their first experience of education was a failure, then why would they consider setting themselves up to fail again; if no one else in their family continued education beyond school-age why should they be different? Gorard and Selwyn argue that these data show that it is possible to predict, at the end of an individual's compulsory schooling, their engagement in lifelong learning. They note that although changes to the school-leaving age has meant that, over time individuals are leaving school with a longer education and higher levels of qualification, the attitudes to education set by the factors described are retained in each cohort. They subsequently argue that the recent focus on the 14–19 agenda will therefore, not change the patterns of participation in lifelong learning; rather, conversely, it has reduced the level of formal adult participation in learning and made it less evenly distributed among different social groups.

It could be argued that if Bourdieu's concepts of capital, habitus and field are correct, then there will be little value in changing the practice of HEIs in order to improve social mobility, as the habitus of non-traditional students will prevent them from succeeding. Indeed, it is this aspect of determinism (e.g. Reay, 2004) which provides much of the criticism of Bourdieu's concept of habitus. However, Bourdieu (1999) also points to the ways in which individuals do strive against current circumstances and postulates that it is when individuals finds themselves in a field which is new to their habitus that the resulting tension produced can generate change and transformation (Reay 2004). Reay also makes the important distinction between the unconscious actions engendered by habitus and the conscious decisions to take different action following reflection and self-questioning.

Rational Decision or Unconscious Action

As described earlier, when Bourdieu considered the effect of habitus on an individual's actions, he argued that the internalisation of ideas about a person's chances of success meant that many of the decisions about engagement with HE are taken unconsciously, in an unexamined process of taking the route expected by an individual based on their habitus. An alternative argument, however, is that this concern with under-representation is actually the middle class patronising the lower socioeconomic classes and that the lower socioeconomic classes are making informed choices about whether to participate or not. Crowther (2000) argues that it is resistance to participation, not barriers which leads to under-representation and that non-participation is a matter of choice.

Hall and Donaldson (1997) considered factors such as parents' education, economic status and early pregnancy in a study of non-participation in adult education in women who had not completed high school education, and found that an important aspect was lack of voice. "The way a woman feels about herself, her self-esteem and self-confidence, and the way she can express herself are significant elements in her decision about whether to participate in adult education" (Hall & Donaldson, 1997, p. 98). Rubenson (1989) found that those who value middle class values are most likely to participate and argued that having an adult education system based on middle class values and contexts was more likely to widen the educational and cultural gaps in society.

Conclusion

This chapter has considered which groups are under-represented in HE and some of the possible reasons for this under-representation based on the theories of Bourdieu. The reasons have been grouped into three major factors—poor education resulting from lack of cultural capital, recruitment practices which reproduce a stratified society and alienation from the dominant culture caused by a dominated habitus—while acknowledging that individuals who do not access HE will have their own combinations and versions of these reasons. Despite differing opinions as to the extent of the under-representation or the extent to which this is linked to social mobility, there does seem to be a recognition that the current system is not yet right for ensuring equality of opportunity for everyone. There is plenty of evidence to demonstrate that Bourdieu's theories of cultural capital and habitus leading to reproduction of a stratified society through the medium of education is applicable to the UK. While there is clearly work to be done during compulsory education to change attitudes to lifelong learning, it is important that the post-compulsory education system is welcoming of a more diverse student body and the recruitment messages need to be backed up with retention practices. There needs to be clear recognition of the difficulties faced by individuals striving to fight against habitus and ensure that educational systems support students in this process of reflection and self-questioning (Reay, 2004). Although there is disagreement as to the extent to which education can improve social mobility and the degree of under-representation of certain classes in HE, there is agreement that there has been an increasing requirement for degree-level education to access many professions (Milburn 2009). For many careers, lack of a degree is a barrier. If WP initiatives in HE are to be successful they need to address the problems of cultural capital, recruitment bias and learner alienation. Unless there is genuine inclusion by recognition of, and meeting the needs of WP students, they are unlikely to be more than aberrations required by universities to fill government-led targets, remaining second-class students outside the dominant framework (Hinton-Smith, 2012).

REFERENCES

Archer, M. (1970). Egalitarianism in English and French educational sociology. *European Journal of Sociology, XI*(1), 116–129.

Archer, L. (2007). Diversity, equality and higher education: A critical reflection on the ab/uses of equity discourse within widening participation. *Teaching in Higher Education, 12*, 635–653. doi:10.1080/13562510701595325.

Archer, L., & Hutchings, M. (2000). 'Bettering yourself'? Discourses of risk, cost and benefit in ethnically diverse, young working-class non-participants' constructions of higher education. *British Journal of Sociology of Education, 21*(4), 555–574.

Archer, L., Hutchings, M., & Ross, A. (2003). *Higher education and social class: Issues of exclusion and inclusion.* Abingdon: RoutledgeFalmer.

Bachan, R. (2013). Students' expectations of debt in UK higher education. *Studies in Higher Education*, 1–26. doi:10.1080/03075079.2012.754859

Berger, P., & Luckmann, T. (1966). *The social construction of reality.* Harmondsworth: Penguin.

Boliver, V. (2013). How fair is access to more prestigious UK universities? *British Journal of Sociology, 64*(2), 344–364. doi:10.1111/1468-4446.12021.

Bourdieu, P. (1976). The school as a conservative force: Scholastic and cultural inequalities. In R. Dale, G. Esland, & M. MacDonald (Eds.), *Schooling and capitalism*. London: Routledge and Keegan Paul in Association with the Open University.

Bourdieu, P. (1984). *Homo Academicus* (P. Collier, Trans.). Stanford: Stanford University Press.

Bourdieu, P. (1986). The forms of capital. In J. Richardson (Ed.), *Handbook of theory and research for the sociology of education* (pp. 241–258). New York: Greenwood.

Bourdieu, P. (1990). *The logic of practice*. Cambridge: Polity Press.

Bourdieu, P. (1993). *The field of cultural production*. Cambridge: Polity Press.

Bourdieu, P. (1999). The contradictions of inheritance. In P. Bourdieu, A. Accardo, G. Balazs, S. Beaud, F. Bonvin, E. Bourdieu, P. Bourgois, S. Broccolichi, P. Champagne, R. Christin, J. P. Faguer, S. Garcia, R. Lenoir, F. Oeuvrard, M. Pialoux, L. Pinto, D. Podalydes, A. Sayad, C. Soulie Loic, & J. D. Wacquant (Eds.), *Weight of the world: Social suffering in contemporary society*. Cambridge: Polity Press.

Bourdieu, P., & Passeron, J. (1990). *Reproduction in education, society and culture* (2nd ed.). London: Sage.

Bowl, M. (2003). *Non-traditional entrants to higher education: 'They talk about people like me'*. Stoke on Trent: Trentham Books.

Callender, C., & Jackson, J. (2005). Does the fear of debt deter students from higher education? *Journal of Social Policy, 34*, 509–540. doi:10.1017/so04727940500913x.

Corver, M. (2010). *Have bursaries influenced choices between universities?* Retrieved 28/10/12, 2012, from http://www.offa.org.uk/wp-content/uploads/2010/09/Have-bursaries-influenced-choices-between-universities-.pdf

Crowther, J. (2000). Participation in adult and community education: A discourse of diminishing returns. *International Journal of Lifelong Education, 19*(6), 479–492.

David, M. (2012). Changing policy discourses on equity and diversity in UK higher education: What is the evidence? In T. Hinton-Smith (Ed.), *Widening participation in higher education: Casting the net wide*. Basingstoke: Palgrave Macmillan.

Dillabough, J. (2004). Class, culture and the 'predicaments of masculine domination': Encountering Pierre Bourdieu. *British Journal of Sociology of Education, 25*(4), 489–506. doi:10.1080/0142569042000236970.

Egerton, M. (2000). Monitoring contemporary student flows and characteristics: Secondary analyses using the Labour Force Survey and the General Household Survey. *Journal of the Royal Statistical Society Series a-Statistics in Society, 163*, 63–80. doi:10.1111/1467-985x.00157.

Gorard, S. (2008). Who is missing from education? *Cambridge Journal of Education, 38*(3), 421–437.

Gorard, S., & Selwyn, N. (2005). What makes a lifelong learner? *Teachers College Record, 107*(6), 1193–1216. doi:10.1111/j.1467-9620.2005.00510.x.

Hall, A. G., & Donaldson, J. F. (1997). An exploratory study of the social and personal dynamics that deter underserved women from participating in adult education activities. *38th Annual Adult Education Research Conference, Proceedings*, 96–101.

Higher Education Funding Council for England, H. (2010). *Trends in young participation in higher education*. Retrieved 28/10/12, 2012, from https://www.hefce.ac.uk/pubs/year/2010/201003/

Hinton-Smith, T. (Ed.). (2012). *Widening participation in higher education: Casting the net wide*. Basingstoke: Palgrave Macmillan.

Hoare, A., & Johnston, R. (2011). Widening participation through admissions policy—A British case study of school and university performance. *Studies in Higher Education, 36*(1), 21–41. doi:10.1080/03075070903414297.

Jenkins, R. (1992). *Pierre Bourdieu*. London: Routledge.

Jones, S. (2013). "Ensure that you stand out from the crowd": A corpus-based analysis of personal statements according to applicants' school type. *Comparative Education Review, 57*(3), 397–423. doi:10.1086/670666.

Knightley, W. M. (2006). Tackling social exclusion through online learning: A preliminary investigation. *Journal of Access Policy and Practice, 4*(1), 20–38.

McClelland, K. (1990). Culmative disadvantage among the highly ambitious. *Sociology of Education, 63*, 102–121.

Milburn, A. (2009). *Unleashing aspiration: The final report of the panel on fair access to the professions*. London: UK Government.

Milburn, A. (2012). *University challenge: How higher education can advance social mobility*. London: Cabinet Office.

Moore, R. (2004). Cultural capital: Objective probability and the cultural arbitrary. *British Journal of Sociology of Education, 25*(4), 445–456. doi:10.1080/0142569042000236943.

Naidoo, R. (2004). Fields and institutional strategy: Bourdieu on the relationship between higher education, inequality and society. *British Journal of Sociology of Education, 25*(4), 457–471. doi:10.1080/0142569042000236952.

Ogg, T., Zimdars, A., & Heath, A. (2009). Schooling effects on degree performance: A comparison of the predictive validity of aptitude testing and secondary school grades at Oxford University. *British Educational Research Journal, 35*(5), 781–807. doi:10.1080/01411920903165611.

PAC, Public Accounts Committee. (2009). *Widening participation in higher education fourth report of session 2008–9* (HC 226). London: The Stationery Office Limited.

Pollard, A. (2008). Preface. In F. Coffield, S. Edward, I. Finlay, A. Hodgson, K. Spours, & R. Steer (Eds.), *Improving learning, skills and inclusion the impact of policy on post-compulsory education preface*. London: Routledge.

Reay, D. (2004). 'It's all becoming a habitus': Beyond the habitual use of habitus in educational research. *British Journal of Sociology of Education, 25*(4), 431–444. doi:10.1080/0142569042000236934.

Robbins, D. (2004). The transcultural transferability of Bourdieu's sociology of education. *British Journal of Sociology of Education, 25*(4), 415–430. doi:10.1080/0142569042000236925.

Rubenson, K. (1989). Sociology of adult education. In S. B. Merriam & P. M. Cunningham (Eds.), *Handbook of adult and continuing education* (pp. 51–69). San Francisco: Jossey-Bass.

Russell Group. (2011). *Informed choices*. 2013, from http://www.russellgroup.ac.uk/media/informed-choices/InformedChoices-latest.pdf

Shiner, M., & Modood, T. (2002). Help or hindrance? Higher education and the route to ethnic equality. *British Journal of Sociology of Education, 23*(2), 209–232. doi:10.1080/01425690220137729.

Sutton Trust. (2004). *Missing 3,000—State schools under-represented in leading universities*. Retrieved 28/10/12, 2012, from http://www.suttontrust.com/research/the-missing-3000/

Swartz, D. (1997). *Culture and power: The sociology of Pierre Bourdieu*. Chicago: The University of Chicago Press.

Tett, L. (2004). Mature working-class students in an 'elite' university: Discourses of risk, choice and exclusion. *Studies in the Education of Adults, 36*(2), 252–264.

Tight, M. (2012). Widening participation: A post-war scorecard. *British Journal of Educational Studies, 60*(3), 211–226. doi:10.1080/00071005.2012.697541.

Universities UK. (2009). *Higher education engagement with schools and colleges: Partnership development*. Retrieved 03/02/2013, 2013, from http://www.universitiesuk.ac.uk/highereducation/Pages/EngagementSchoolsColleges.aspx

Watson, K. (2007). Private higher education. *International Journal of Educational Development, 27*(4), 476–477. doi:10.1016/j.ijedudev.2005.10.007.

Woodley, A., & Wilson, J. (2002). British higher education and its older clients. *Higher Education, 44*(3–4), 329–347. doi:10.1023/a:1019857315244.

Yorke, M. (2012). Widening participation in universities in England and Wales: Is there a connection with honours degree achievement? In T. Hinton-Smith (Ed.), *Widening participation in higher education: Casting the net wide*. Basingstoke: Palgrave Macmillan.

CHAPTER 2

Understanding Foundation Year Provision

Steve Leech, Catherine A. Marshall, and Geoff Wren

INTRODUCTION

In the 2011 Government White Paper "Students at the Heart of the System" foundation year programmes were suggested as one of the options for improving access to Higher Education (HE) amongst the least well off young people and adults, and as a means for HEIs to engage with the National Scholarship Programme (Cable, 2011, p. 61). The Minister of State for Universities and Science further suggested that foundation-level provision will be instrumental in maintaining widening participation (WP) and access to HE (Willetts, 2010). However, there appears to be very little clarity about the scope and nature of foundation-level provision within the UK and an urgent need for discussion about how the foundation sector can fulfil the expectations being placed upon it.

The need for mechanisms to support WP in HE is widely accepted. Concerns regarding the potential impact on WP groups (OFFA, 2012), especially adult learners (NIACE, 2011) in the light of the new HE funding model are based on significant bodies of research that suggest that

S. Leech (✉) • C.A. Marshall • G. Wren
Foundation Centre, University of Durham, Pelaw House, Leazes Road, Durham
DH1 1TA, UK

WP students are the most likely to experience negative impact of higher fees. It has, for example, been well documented that financial concerns represent a significant barrier to WP groups entering HE (Pollard et al., 2008). Such groups are often geographically grounded, due to family and financial responsibilities (Pollard et al., 2008; Fuller & Patton, 2007) and therefore less able to relocate in order to access institutions with lower course fees. Further, students from lower socio-economic groups are inclined to be risk averse in their approach to borrowing (Callender & Jackson, 2005), with additional regional variation in debt aversion that may exacerbate the current regional imbalance in HE participation (Whitely in Baker, 2011).

This chapter outlines some of the initiatives to widen participation which are either in use or may be considered for use in the UK. It is not meant to be a comprehensive analysis of WP in the UK, but rather a way of locating foundation programme activity in WP in general and the Durham Foundation Programme specifically in the UK foundation programme profile. As will be explored in a later chapter, much of the WP has focused on recruitment rather than ensuring that the students' experience is appropriate to their background. For example, the Office for Fair Access reported that the estimated spend on fair access initiatives by universities for 2013–14 was, on average, 26.5% of the extra fee income above the basic fee, with 18.8% focused on bursaries for students, 4.2% on outreach activities but only 3.5% on retention activities (OFFA, 2012).

The most common mechanism currently utilised by English universities to widen participation is to offer financial support in the form of bursaries or scholarships (OFFA, 2012). There is little evidence, however, that bursaries alter students' behaviour with regard to choice of university (Corver, 2010). Other WP initiatives which address recruitment issues focus on outreach activities and admissions processes; the former to increase the numbers of applications from under-represented groups and the latter to convert those applications to offers of places (Milburn, 2012; OFFA, 2012). Outreach activities include those which raise aspirations, improve students' attainment while still in pre-university education, and increase awareness of HE by the use of summer schools, school visits to university campuses and mentoring programmes. Changes to admissions processes are less widely employed, with some universities considering contextual data alongside qualifications, for example, the likelihood of students from a school to achieve good A level grades, and others diversifying admissions criteria (OFFA, 2012).

Does Widening Provision Lead to Widened Participation?

The extent to which WP in HE will affect social mobility is dependent on the strength of the link between education and social mobility. An economic model of social mobility proposed by Blanden et al. (2004) correlates declining social mobility rates with educational inequality, which has led to an emphasis on education as the major tool for overcoming the problem. Goldthorpe's (2013) alternative model, however, suggests that changes in educational policy will have little effect on either absolute or relative social mobility rates. Absolute social mobility rates have, in the past, been affected by changes in employment and, as a result, class structures, and Lucas's model of effectively maintained inequality indicates that advantaged parents will use economic resource to maintain the inequality (Lucas, 2001). This is not a new argument; Neelsen (1975) argued that social inequality is structurally determined and is likely to be maintained by class succession, institutional differentiation and devaluation of education, and that focussing on education as a means for change was unlikely to produce anything other than marginal improvements. Most researchers do accept the role of education in social mobility, for example, Boliver asserts that "mass participation in HE is widely considered to be crucial not only in the continued international economic competitiveness of industrialised nations, but also to the promotion of social justice and social mobility within modern societies." (2011, p. 229). Increasing the number of places available in HE is unlikely to be a simple solution to the issue of inequality of opportunity, however, as there will be other barriers preventing under-represented groups accessing those places and subsequently accessing professions which confer wealth and status.

Boliver questions the assumption that HE expansion alone can reduce socio-economic inequalities (2011)—the assumption that widening provision will lead to widened participation. This assumption arose out of modernisation theory which predicted that as industrialised nations required workers to be more educated, the expansion of education would lead to educational equalisation (Parsons & Platt, 1970; Treiman, 1970). Treiman argues that the free mass education systems more likely to be found in industrialised countries mean that in such situations, opportunities would become more meritocratic and based on education rather than financial resource (1970). However, evidence indicated that this was not the case and that inequalities in the secondary educational system remained (Halsey, 1980). In order to explain this discrepancy, Raftery and Hout (1993) formulated the hypothesis of Maximally Maintained Inequality (MMI) which was later expanded on by Lucas (2001) to encompass Effectively Maintained Inequality (EMI). What these hypotheses contend is that when educational opportunities are expanded, it will be those from more socio-economically advantaged backgrounds who will avail themselves of the opportunities, and only when the majority of young people from these groups are engaged with HE will further expansion benefit those from less advantaged backgrounds.

Boliver (2011) conducted a study to test whether the predictions made by MMI and EMI were upheld in the empirical data for the UK HE. She tracked the increase in HE participation by social class and found that between 1960 and 1995, there was an increase in probability of participation in HE for all classes, but that the relative likelihood of participation between service class (NS-SEC 1 and 2) and working class remained about the same (change of 0.16 in probability for service class to access HE compared with 0.20 for working class) whereas the greatest change was in the probability of someone from intermediate class participating (change of 0.34). Boliver makes the point that this expansion for the intermediate class "occurred only after the enrolment rate for the service class had reached 'saturation' point" (2011, p. 238). Having considered the quantitative increases in participation in HE, Boliver then analysed the qualitative differences in whether students were enrolled in degree programmes and the type of institution in which they were enrolled. The results showed that inequalities in enrolment in both degree programmes and at "old" universities were maintained, demonstrating the same class inequalities as had been prevalent in 1960 (i.e. those from the service class were much more likely to be enrolled on degrees and be enrolled at an old university than those from the intermediate class and working class.) There is an even greater inequality when institution is considered; in 1960 the difference in probability of attending an old university from the service class was about 0.18 greater than from the working class; in 1995 that difference had increased to 0.25.

What these studies indicate is that more needs to be done to recruit under-represented groups into HE beyond simply making more places available. The rest of the chapter considers some of these recruitment practices.

Sutton Trust's Range of Initiatives

In 2010, the Sutton Trust commissioned an analysis of various methods of WP. The initiatives were evaluated in terms of cost-benefit ratio by comparing the estimated cost of implementing the scheme with the estimated increase in lifetime earnings for those involved in the initiative. The report provides a comprehensive description of a wide-ranging set of mechanisms to widen participation which could be utilised in the UK, and some key features include the following:

- Independent career advice services reached over half a million students but was costly, and its effect on the students' anticipated lifelong earnings (prospects) was relatively small;
- University access programmes and summer schools at leading universities reached fewer students but the anticipated benefits to the students were the greatest of all the strategies;
- Teacher training and awareness raising activities potentially affected a moderate number of students and their impact on student prospects was similarly moderate;
- Initiatives involving, for example, interventions with early years and primary school children, supporting able, secondary school children with low-income parents, or providing them with "enrichment" opportunities were applied to relatively large numbers of students in total, but showed relatively unimpressive effects on those students' prospects.

Overall, direct involvement of universities working with the students showed most promise. (This is not to say that other strategies are worthless; it may be that, in combination with university provision, they have the potential to add to the overall success of the endeavour although this is unlikely to be significant if used alone.)

All the initiatives in the analysis were directed at improving initial education or improving the progression from initial education to university and as such would be directed at individuals who were currently in education—either still in school or at Sixth Form college or a Further Education (FE) college—in other words, a captive audience. Even if a large number of these initiatives were implemented immediately, there would still be a large number of non-traditional students who are currently outside the education system who would not benefit. A further consideration is that none of these initiatives address the issue of learner alienation in the university context. The Milburn Report (2012) indicates that the lack of focus on retention activities means that the rate of improvement in retention has been slow and the variation between different universities with regard to retention rates remains high and that some non-traditional student groups are more likely to drop out of university. This means that non-traditional students are perceived to pose a risk to both the university they enrol with and the state which invests in them (Leathwood & O'Connell, 2003).

For non-traditional students who do not have the traditional A level qualification to access university, there are generally three routes to a degree level education: The Open University, Access courses or Foundation Programmes. A very small number of institutions are willing to take students without equivalent qualifications. For example, a study into WP explored whether lowering entry qualifications and accepting non-traditional entry qualifications would adversely influence the performance and progression statistics of institutions by considering student outcomes. The results concluded that neither performance nor progression were affected by entry qualifications once other factors such as module load and the subject taken by the student were allowed for. They found that, on the whole, students taking Business or Social Science degrees tended to do less well in terms of performance but that this was less marked in students with vocational or no formal qualifications, who were mature and had relevant work experience (Houston, Knox, & Rimmer, 2007). This is an unusual model however, and most institutions expect students to do some preparation for university level study.

ROUTES TO HIGHER EDUCATION FOR THOSE WITHOUT TRADITIONAL QUALIFICATIONS

The Open University

Woodley (2012) analysed the role of the Open University on WP in the UK as its stated aim when it began delivering HE in 1971 was to be "open as to people" (2012, p. 51) meaning that the aim was to make university education available to all people. It was distinctive in that it required no entry qualifications, delivered its programmes at a distance on a part-time basis so that students could continue to work and live at home and the credit-based system allowed a flexible approach to learning. On its inception, the Open University only had around 25% women enrolments, but this has steadily increased to just over 60% in 2009. However, this is against a background of a general increase in female participation in HE, with little or no special case being argued for the Open University as particularly championing women's participation (Woodley & Wilson, 2002). In fact, as previously discussed in Chap. 1, there is a good argument to be made for considering men as the under-represented group (Gorard, 2008).

The Open University originally targeted mature students, setting a lower age limit of 21 for enrolment, which has since been removed, and the median age for Open University students has been consistently around the early 30s. Although the median age has remained constant, this does not reflect the changing pattern of student age in the Open University—in the last 10 years, the proportion of enrolments for students in the age group 30–39 has been decreasing. At the same time, the number of enrolments from students under the age of 25 has been increasing, so that in 2009 nearly 25% of enrolments were from students aged under 25 (Woodley, 2012).

As with gender, the rates of Black and Minority Ethnic students have increased in the Open University, but this is against a backdrop of general increase in HE participation in this group. The data does not show that students with disabilities are more likely to engage with the Open University rather than standard institutions, with a much greater percentage (about 8.5%) of new enrolments in full-time HE being students with disabilities than in the Open University (just under 4%). The raw data does not give a picture of the range and effect of disabilities on students' ability to engage with HE, however, and there may be a qualitative difference in the types of disabilities experienced by Open University students compared with other HEIs (Woodley, 2012).

The Open University does not require students to have previous qualifications and consequently, a large proportion of the students do not possess qualifications which would normally gain them access to HE. This is balanced, however, by the fact there is a much larger proportion of students with previous HE experience. Consequently, when trying to measure how successful the Open University is at WP, Woodley describes the situation as "rather confusing" (2012, p. 59). Where the Open University is clearly having an effect on WP is in improving the representation in HE of people from lower social classes; Woodley cites that of those students who declared parental background, 50% were described as working class (2012).

Access to Higher Education Diploma

Access to HE programmes are specifically designed for those without traditional qualifications as a preparation for HE (QAA, 2013) and are usually offered by FE Colleges. They are characterised as being focused on vocational degrees and consequently are more likely to provide routes to non-elite universities than other forms of university preparation. This is particularly true for female students accessing nursing, social work and so on which have low pay, low status and long hours, and tend to mirror traditional, stereotypical female roles, rather than providing opportunities to explore new identities (Jackson, 2004 in (Hinton-Smith, 2012). There is research which shows that universities report higher retention rates with A level students when compared with Access students and consequently elite universities are reluctant to offer places to Access students, preferring to fill their places with those students who are more likely to complete their course (Hinton-Smith, 2012).

There also appears to be issues with Access students' approaches to studying. Richardson (1994a, 1994b, 1994c, 1995) conducted a series of studies into the approaches to studying adopted by mature students and although the results showed that mature students developed desirable study methods, one aspect of the study indicated that mature students on Access courses were less likely to adopt desirable approaches to studying than other mature students (Hayes, King, & Richardson, 1997). As the authors recognise, the study does not prove causation, however, they suggest that the distinctive approach to education embodied in Access courses may be "inculcating attitudes, approaches and orientations to studying which are inconsistent with those of the majority of students in higher education" (1997, p. 28). They report that many Access students either do not progress to HE, or withdraw early in the course and they suggest that the cultural differences may provide a partial explanation.

Osborne, Leopold and Ferrie (1997) conducted a study comparing the performance of students with traditional and non-traditional qualifications admitted to the University of Stirling. They found that of all non-school entrants, Business and Technology Education Council (BTEC) students, performed consistently below average and that Access students studying Maths and Science were more likely to perform less well than other Access students. They found, however, that students entering from the University's own Access course performed only slightly lower than students entering with General Certificate of Education (GCE) A levels and concluded that students were more likely to perform well in HE if the University had a strong influence on the execution of the Access course, particularly if the course was delivered in HE rather than FE.

Other Vocation Provision in Further Education: Foundation Degrees

It is important to note the difference between foundation degrees and foundation programmes. Foundation degrees are distinct from Year 0 foundation programmes as they are vocational qualifications designed for students who are working in the area in which they wish to gain their qualification and who take the first two years of their degree with a Further Education Institution (FEI). They can then complete their degree by taking a further two years at a Higher Education Institution.

David (2012) described a study investigating HE in FE collaborations and whether these initiatives lead to a seamless system of tertiary education. The study showed, however, that "institutions, staff and students treat FE and HE as separate enterprises, affecting the practices of students and tutors at various stages in the student lifecycle and the imagined futures at the end of college study" (p. 25). This may well reflect the different communities of practice found in the different types of institutions. Certainly, a study to explore the transition from vocational education and training showed that students entering HE with vocational qualifications were less likely to gain a place and to keep it beyond their first year (David, 2012).

Foundation Programmes

The desire for control over pre-degree courses has led to a number of universities developing their own foundation programmes to provide an alternative to the Access model. A further incentive was provided by the increasing competition for student numbers, by new universities in particular, and some institutions started becoming dependent on recruiting WP students, often with lower entry qualifications and requiring greater educational support. Retention rates for such students were lower due to social issues related to lack of cultural capital and practical factors such as the need to take up paid work (Ainley, 2002). During this reversal in numbers, in the mid to late 1990s, universities began to develop foundation programmes as a mechanism to prepare such students for university.

OUTLINE OF A STUDY TO COMPARE FOUNDATION PROGRAMMES IN THE UK

There appears to be very little clarity about the scope and nature of foundation level provision within the UK, and there appear to be very few studies of this relatively new type of provision. In order to produce a national picture of foundation provision, in July 2011 Durham University's Foundation Centre commissioned a review of the data available to the public on foundation courses, from the websites of 127 universities throughout the UK. Foundation provision for both home and European Union (EU) students and overseas status students were assessed. The main data sources were the websites produced by the HEIs, with each provider being researched for both home and EU and overseas provision. The sample included universities that based foundation years in house, and those provided in partnership with FE colleges. Of the 127 universities analysed, 76 institutions offered some form of foundation year programme for home and EU students and 103 for overseas/international students.

HOME AND EUROPEAN UNION (EU) PROVISION

The 76 institutions offering a home and EU student foundation year included representation from each university affiliation group: Russell Group, 1994 Group, Million+, University Alliance and institutions which were unaffiliated (Table 2.1).

A majority (51 of 76) of the universities offering foundation year programmes for home students based these entirely within academic departments with no involvement from outside providers (e.g. FE colleges), and no bespoke Foundation Centre in which teaching might be based. A further 11 universities offered a range of home foundation year programmes that were taught by a combination of academic departments

Table 2.1 Foundation year provision by university group

Affiliation	Number of universities by affiliation offering foundation programmes	Number of universities in affiliation group	Percentage of universities offering foundation programmes by affiliation group (%)
Russell Group	10	20	50
1994 Group	12	18	67
Million+	19	27	70
University Alliance	18	23	78
Unaffiliated	17	39	45

and external providers. In these universities, different programmes were taught at different locations and by different delivery organisations (rather than a university and, for example, a private sector provider delivering a course jointly).

In total, 18 institutions offered at least one foundation year programme through an FE college and 11 universities offered a combination of in house and college-based programmes. Among these 11 institutions, Computing Science was the most common foundation year programme to be offered through an FE College, rather than the university, and by contrast, programmes in Engineering were most likely to be offered in house by these institutions. The FE colleges involved in programme delivery, in these cases, were all located off site (i.e. outside the university campus in question), though the majority of these were relatively local to the universities. There were seven universities which offered foundation year programmes through FE colleges and Sixth Form colleges alone (i.e. there was no in house provision). The majority of the colleges involved in delivering these programmes were based off site. In five of these cases, programmes were delivered by no more than two separate FE colleges although in one case the university worked with six colleges and in another, eight.

Only three universities provided their foundation year programmes for home students through a bespoke Foundation Centre. In each case, these Foundation Centres were organised by the university in question; there was no evidence of outsourcing of these centres to the private sector. The four Scottish Access courses researched were based exclusively in Centre for Lifelong Learning facilities (although these sometimes had different names). In the case of universities with specialist Foundation Centres, teaching took place in those Centres, rather than academic departments.

The majority of home provision was therefore, based within academic departments and comprised Year 0 of an integrated course of academic study, in which students progressed to Year 1 within the same academic department. In some cases, the foundation year was relatively broad, which would then enable students to choose from a range of more closely defined subjects at Year 1. In these cases, progression was within a faculty, rather than a specific academic department.

Programmes based entirely within academic departments/faculties were usually offered as part of a four-year integrated programme (particularly in the case of Science and Engineering courses), and therefore led by members of academic staff within the subject area concerned. However, it was unclear whether courses would be taught by full-time academics or by session teachers, such as PhD students or postdoctoral researchers. Courses based in FE colleges were typically taught by members of college staff, rather than university academics, although it was unclear whether there was any *ad hoc* guest teaching by university academics within these courses. Courses based in Foundation Centres were taught by specialist staff within those locations; again, however, it was not clear whether there was any "guesting" of academic staff within these programmes, or if students were required to attend any occasional teaching within academic departments.

The vast majority of programmes offered were in Sciences, Engineering, Computing, Art and Design or Medicine, with only a very small number of institutions offering Year 0 courses in Social Sciences or Humanities (see Table 2.2). The four Scottish Access courses were not subject-specific and are therefore, not included in the analysis.

Table 2.2 Availability of foundation year by academic discipline

Academic discipline	Number of institutions offering pathway
Engineering & Technology	52
Sciences & Mathematics	49
Computing	22
Art & Design	21
Humanities & Social Sciences	12
Business & Management	9
Medicine	8
Sport Sciences	6
Law	5

A small number of programmes lay outside these areas including Health and Social Studies, Games and Animation, Motor Sports, Film and Television Production and a bespoke Foundation Year for the Visually-Impaired. Two institutions had programmes which were more generalist in nature.

The majority (61) of institutions offered five or fewer individual foundation year programmes/routes, and only four institutions offered more than ten individual foundation year programmes/routes. Although there was no direct correlation between university group affiliation and the number of programmes offered, there was some tendency for Russell Group universities to offer a higher number of programmes on average than those in other groups. Programmes in these institutions were often more subject-specific than elsewhere (e.g. a foundation year in three or four separate engineering disciplines, rather than simply a single foundation year in engineering).

About half (34) of the institutions did not provide details of course structures. However, where that information was available, many foundation year programmes were based around a 120-credit model in which 60 credits were studied per semester. The number of modules that students were required to study differed between institutions, and between course offerings within the same institution; typical course structures were 2–4 modules per semester (with each module being worth 15–30 credits), resulting in 4–8 modules in total. A number of programmes required students to complete study skills modules as part of Year 0; however, in most cases the majority of content appeared to be subject-specific. There was little cross-sector standardisation concerning the proportion of Year 0 dedicated to study skills.

Modes of delivery for foundation year programmes among home students were usually full-time. Part-time delivery was offered at two universities. It is possible that a number of other universities would consider accepting Year 0 students on a part-time basis, but this was not explicitly detailed within university websites. Scottish Access courses were delivered part-time in the evenings in order to enable students to continue in full-time employment. Specific weekly contact hours were rarely detailed on university websites, and it appears likely that different courses had different contact hours depending on the subject studied. For those ten institutions based in England which did provide details of contact hours, the hours varied between 12 and 20 per week.

Entry requirements for foundation year programmes were extremely diverse for those aged under 21, although most institutions specified both a minimum and maximum points score required to apply for Year 0. In all but eight cases, entry requirements were based around meeting Universities and Colleges Admissions Service (UCAS) points scores. Although there was no absolute and direct correlation between university ranking and UCAS tariff points required for entry to Year 0, there was a tendency for newer universities to demand fewer points with this variation ranging from 40 points for a lower ranked university and 240 points for a higher ranked institution. Some (though not all) of the research-focused universities intended their Year 0 programmes to be studied only by high-achieving students who had taken unrelated A levels (e.g. a Science applicant who had studied History and English at A level). In these cases, students were required to achieve 300 or more UCAS points (around ABB at A level).

Eight institutions did not require any UCAS points in order to qualify for entry to Year 0 courses. In these cases, applicants were evaluated on more subjective qualities (such as demonstration of clear interest in the subject matter of the course). These institutions were spread across all of the different types of university affiliation; they did not all belong to, for example, the Russell Group.

There were also some notable differences between different programmes offered within the same institution (28 of the 57 institutions offering more than one foundation year programme listed different entry requirements for different courses); in one case, requirement ranged from 80 to 180 UCAS points within the same institution. This was mostly on the basis of subject type, with applicants for Medicine routinely required to have BBB or higher at A level, and entry was more conditional upon meeting eligibility criteria relating to socio-economic background, whereas applicants for Engineering courses were rarely required to achieve such qualifications prior to Year 0 entry. Art and Design courses usually required students to have passed one A level and to have a portfolio of some work available for assessment by foundation year recruiters. General Certificate of Secondary Education (GCSE) English and Maths (at minimum grade C) were also required by most providers for all foundation year programmes, irrespective of applicants' UCAS A level points' tallies.

Mature entrants (i.e. those over the age of 21) were rarely required to have formal Level 3 qualifications, although it was usually expected that there would be evidence of prior exposure to the academic subject in question (e.g. gained through previous employment), and good standards of literacy and numeracy were also expected. They were typically interviewed in order to assess their suitability for Year 0 programmes. Entry criteria for these students was therefore much more subjective and at the discretion of individual universities. Mature entrants were expected not to have studied for degree-level qualifications previously.

In all cases, students were considered ineligible for the foundation year if their existing qualifications would gain entry to Year 1 within the same institution. Eligibility for Medicine foundation years was strongly related to WP. Ten institutions did not admit "near miss" Year 1 applicants to Year 0. Russell and 1994 Group universities were least likely to offer "near miss" Year 1 applicants places on foundation year programmes; this was particularly so where programmes were intended for high-achievers with less relevant A levels, rather than those with low UCAS scores. Many new universities did not state whether "near miss" applicants for Year 1 would be offered places at Year 0 instead; however, as these institutions often required relatively low UCAS points scores to enter foundation year courses, this may be the case. As the data on this area was often incomplete (in 51 cases, there was no definitive statement to determine whether "near miss" students would be considered for Year 0 entry), it was difficult to quantify the precise number of institutions that would be prepared to admit potential Year 1 applicants to Year 0.

In all cases, assessment was undertaken through a combination of examinations, coursework (essays and other short written assignments) and, in the case of Science, Engineering and some Computing programmes, laboratory work.

The information about student experience was sporadic and in many cases not detailed at all, but there was little to suggest that pastoral support, accommodation arrangements and student status and access to facilities was significantly different from that offered to Year 1 undergraduates. Those based in FE colleges had mixed access, ranging from full and equal access to all university facilities, to reduced library and sports facilities for Year 1 students. Information about access to university facilities, however, was not always available for courses outsourced to FE colleges; it was therefore difficult to draw firm conclusions about this from the desk data alone.

International Provision

According to *Patterns and Trends in UK Higher Education 2013* (UUK, 2013), there were around 2.5 million students registered to study in the UK's 163 HEIs during the period 2011–12. A relatively small but rising proportion of these students come from non-EU countries. In 2003–04, the percentage was 8.6% of all students but by 2011–12, it had risen to 12.1% —approximately 300,000 students. This represents around 13% of the global market and is estimated to be worth £10.2 billion to the UK economy in tuition fees and living expenses alone. There is also recognition that "international students enhance the UK's cultural life and broaden the educational experience of the students they study alongside" (UUK, 2013, p. 11). It is assumed that the UK government and universities will continue to strive for a larger share of this market.

The largest numbers of non-EU students come, in descending order by numbers, from Asia (mainly China and India), Africa, North America, the Middle East and then South America and the single biggest market is for those doing a first degree—125,000 students. Disregarding North America, most of the students wishing to pursue a first degree come from countries whose own education system is deemed incompatible with the UK system—only 12 years instead of 13 years (see UCAS). Thus, many of the 125,000 have qualifications recognised as below A level and not sufficient for direct entry to undergraduate programmes and consequently need to take some form of a foundation year. International foundation programmes then are generally designed to fill the gap between an applicant's current level of qualifications and those needed to enter a Bachelors degree at a UK (or other EU) institution. In short, they are designed to make the successful student eligible for admission but most will try and offer more: improved language proficiency, admission to university of your choice, a specific set of background knowledge and skills and a smooth transition (e.g. culture shock).

Given the size of the market and the diversity of needs, unsurprisingly there are many different types of foundation programmes. Some, for example may contain English language elements, others may not; some may provide generic preparation, whilst others are tailored for a specific field (e.g. Business, Law or Engineering); some are only for international students while others combine both home and international. Most of them tend to be of one academic year duration but some are fast track. The qualifications needed to enter vary broadly but basically you will need to have successfully completed 12 years of basic education somewhere in the world and have a certain level of English language proficiency (at least 5.5 on the International English Language Testing System (IELTS), for example). Although, for the time being, the majority of programmes are designed and delivered by UK HE and FE institutions (particularly in the 'selecting' universities) some of the world's largest and most established private education providers have captured around 40% of the market. Among the most notable are: Kaplan, INTO, Study Group (including Bellerby's), Cambridge Education Group (Foundation Campus) and Navitas.

MOTIVATIONS FOR DEVELOPING FOUNDATION PROGRAMMES

In order to explore the data provided in the report, the information was analysed with respect to the university rankings and the analysis is shown in Table 2.3 below. To calculate the relative positions in the rankings, three different rankings were used for the year 2010: *Times*, *Complete University Guide* and *Guardian*. An average of these rankings was used to place universities in the first quartile (top 25% of rankings) through to the bottom quartile (lowest 25% of rankings). There is a clear differ-

Table 2.3 Use of foundation programmes by universities by ranking

Quartile in rankings	Total	% with home foundation	% with international foundation
Q1—upper	26	46.2 (n=12)	84.6 (n=22)
Q2—second	29	75.9 (n=22)	93.1 (n=27)
Q3—third	30	60.0 (n=18)	80.0 (n=24)
Q4—lowest	26	73.1 (n=19)	92.3 (n=24)

ence between the upper quartile and the rest of the institutions in terms of whether they provide a home foundation programme, whereas there is no difference in the percentages of institutions providing international foundation programmes for comparison.

Top ranking universities usually have selecting departments, which means that they have a greater number of suitable applicants for each place available, whereas universities further down the rankings are more likely to be recruiting institutions; the implication being that they have to work to attract students to ensure that quotas are met. There are likely to be two different motivations for developing foundation programmes: for some recruiting universities, foundation programmes enable them to take students who were intending to go to university, but who have not achieved high enough A level grades, that is, deepening participation and for selecting universities the purpose is more likely to be to increase the diversity of student applicants, by including those who have not taken the A level route and consequently widen participation.

Modelling the Different Foundation Programmes

In order to capture the variation of foundation year programme delivery nationally, we analysed the data to group programmes into models based on two important areas of variation:

1. Entry requirements: The primary modelling criterion was the entry requirements for each foundation year programme. This criterion also provided information on whether mature students were encouraged to apply. A programme which only specified UCAS tariff points as an entry requirement without reference to mature student entry was deemed to be focusing on attracting students with recent A level study, which we are referring to as deepening participation. Where mature students were mentioned as not requiring the same UCAS tariff points as under 21s, the implication is that the programme mixes mature students with those with recent A level study. No requirement for UCAS tariff points indicates a focus on WP beyond students with recent A level study.
2. Structural locus of delivery: The secondary modelling criterion is the structural locus of delivery, that is, whether the foundation year programme is delivered in academic departments, FE colleges or a specialist centre. In turn, this provides insight into student

Table 2.4 Matrix of modelled delivery combinations (Number of foundation year programmes using each combination) (Marshall & Leech, 2011)

		Entry requirements		
		UCAS points required for all age groups	UCAS points required for <21, but not >21	No UCAS points required
Where taught	Academic departments	Model 1 (n=21)	Model 2 (n=20)	Model 3 (n=10)
	Specialist centre	Model 4 (n=2)	Model 5 (n=0)	Model 6 (n=6)
	Academic department and FE college	Model 7 (n=2)	Model 8 (n=6)	Model 9 (n=2)
	FE college	Model 10 (n=1)	Model 11 (n=3)	Model 12 (n=3)

experience. For students in academic departments, the student support may be generic, that is, the same as Year 1 students, whereas students in a specialist centre are likely to receive tailored support, and those in an FE setting may receive student support from either the FE college or the university's generic systems.

The model, therefore, provides 12 potential combinations that are identified in Table 2.4. Of the 12 possible combinations 11 were found to be in use.

The Foundation Programme at Durham University is a Category 6 model, where there is no A level grade profile or UCAS points entry requirement and students are taught in a dedicated centre. This model is used by six institutions and five of them deliver courses with wide ranging progression routes. Durham is the only English institution which uses this model; there are four similar instances of provision in Scotland and one in Wales. This model is focused on WP for students who have not recently studied at A level, addressing the issue of inadequate initial education and recruitment processes. The centre-based approach allows for tailored support to help overcome issues of alienation.

Conclusion

The work of the Office for Fair Access (OFFA) has led to a range of recruitment initiatives, frequently based on bursaries or fee waivers, to increase the proportions of non-traditional students in universities. Evidence indicates, however, that students may need more than purely financial support gain access to university and certainly those who do not have appropriate qualifications will need to make use of alternative routes. It is important to have a range of initiatives as the issue is complex and there will not be a single solution for the wide range of non-traditional students. In terms of provision for non-traditional mature students, foundation programmes can offer routes that overcome recruitment bias, allow for inadequate initial education and can also address issues of alienation. Within the foundation programme provision, the Durham Foundation Centre is quite unique in that it offers routes to all departments in the University, delivers the Year 0 teaching in a central unit with dedicated teaching staff and does not require any formal qualifications for entry.

References

Ainley, P. (2002). Capitalism and social progress, the future of society in a global economy. *Journal of Education Policy, 17*(5), 603–604. doi:10.1080/02680930210158348.

Baker, S. (2011). Fee-averse Northerners could leave their local universities out of pocket. *Times Higher Education*. http://www.timeshighereducation.co.uk/story.asp?storycode=416877.

Blanden, J., Goodman, A., Gregg, P., & Machin, S. (2004). Changes in intergenerational mobility in Britain. In M. Corak (Ed.), *Generational income mobility*. Cambridge: Cambridge University Press.

Boliver, V. (2011). Expansion, differentiation, and the persistence of social class inequalities in British higher education. *Higher Education, 61*(3), 229–242. doi:10.1007/s10734-010-9374-y.

Cable, V. (2011). Students at the heart of the system. London: The Stationery Office Limited. Retrieved from https://www.gov.uk/government/uploads/system/uploads/attachment_data/file/32409/11-944-higher-education-students-at-heart-of-system.pdf.

Callender, C., & Jackson, J. (2005). Does the fear of debt deter students from higher education? *Journal of Social Policy, 34*, 509–540. doi:10.1017/so04727940500913x.

Corver, M. (2010). *Have bursaries influenced choices between universities?* Retrieved October 28, 2012, from http://www.offa.org.uk/wpcontent/uploads/2010/09/Have-bursaries-influenced-choices-between-universities-.pdf.

David, M. (2012). Changing policy discourses on equity and diversity in UK higher education: What is the evidence? In T. Hinton-Smith (Ed.), *Widening participation in higher education: Casting the net wide*. Basingstoke: Palgrave Macmillan.

Fuller, A., & Paton, K. (2007). *Barriers to participation in higher education? Depends who you ask and how.* Paper presented at the British Educational Research Association Annual Conference, Institute of Education, University of London, 5–8 September 2007.

Goldthorpe, J. H. (2013). Understanding- and misunderstanding: Social mobility in Britain: The entry of the economists, the confusion of politicians and the limits of educational policy. *Journal of Social Policy, 42*, 431–450. doi: 10.1017/s004727941300024x.

Gorard, S. (2008). Who is missing from education? *Cambridge Journal of Education, 38*(3), 421–437.

Halsey, A. H. (1980). Education can compensate. *New Society, 51*(903), 172–174.

Hayes, K., King, E., & Richardson, J. T. E. (1997). Mature students in higher education 3. Approaches to studying in access students. *Studies in Higher Education, 22*(1), 19–31. doi:10.1080/03075079712331381111.

Hinton-Smith, T. (Ed.). (2012). *Widening participation in higher education: Casting the net wide*. Basingstoke: Palgrave Macmillan.

Houston, M., Knox, H., & Rimmer, R. (2007). Wider access and progression among full-time students. *Higher Education, 53*(1), 107–146. doi:10.1007/s10734-005-3177-6.

Leathwood, C., & O'Connell, P. (2003). 'It's a struggle': The construction of the 'new student' in higher education. *Journal of Education Policy, 18*(6), 597–615. doi:10.1080/0268093032000145863.

Lucas, S. R. (2001). Effectively maintained inequality: Education transitions, track mobility, and social background effects. *American Journal of Sociology, 106*(6), 1642–1690. doi:10.1086/321300.

Marshall, C., & Leech, S. (2011). Comparison of Foundation Programme Models in the UK. *Proceedings of the Foundation Year Network Annual Conference*, Sheffield.

Milburn, A. (2012). *University challenge: How higher education can advance social mobility*. London: Cabinet Office.

Neelsen, J. P. (1975). Education and social mobility. *Comparative Education Review, 19*(1), 129–143. doi:10.1086/445813.

NIACE. (2011). HE White Paper Response Friday, July 1, 2011—15:50 http://www.niace.org.uk/news/he-white-paper-%3D-niace-response.

OFFA (2012). *Office for Fair Access Annual report and accounts* 2011–12. London: The Stationery Office.

Osborne, M., Leopold, J., & Ferrie, A. (1997). Does access work? The relative performance of access students at a Scottish university. *Higher Education, 33*(2), 155–176. doi:10.1023/a:1002927816754.

Parsons, T., & Platt, G. M. (1970). Age, social structure and socialization in higher education. *Sociology of Education, 43*(1), 1–37. doi:10.2307/2112057.

Pollard, E., Bates, P., Hunt, W., & Bellis, A. (2008). *University is not just for young people: working adults' perceptions of and orientation to higher education*, Institute for Employment Studies, DIUS Research Report 08 06, London.

QAA. (2013). Access to higher education. From http://www.accesstohe.ac.uk/Pages/Default.aspx

Raftery, A. E., & Hout, M. (1993). Maximally maintained inequality—Expansion, reform, and opportunity in Irish education, 1921–75. *Sociology of Education, 66*(1), 41–62. doi:10.2307/2112784.

Richardson, J. T. E. (1994a). Cultural specificity of approaches to studying in higher education—A literature survey. *Higher Education, 27*(4), 449–468. doi:10.1007/bf01384904.

Richardson, J. T. E. (1994b). Mature students in higher education—1. A literature survey on approaches to studying. *Studies in Higher Education, 19*(3), 309–325. doi:10.1080/03075079412331381900.

Richardson, J. T. E. (1994c). Mature students in higher education—Academic performance and intellectual ability. *Higher Education, 28*(3), 373–386. doi:10.1007/bf01383723.

Richardson, J. T. E. (1995). Mature students in higher education—Academic performance and intellectual ability. 2. An investigation into approach to studying and academic performance. *Studies in Higher Education, 20*(1), 5–17. doi:10.1080/03075079512331381760.

Sutton Trust. (2010). *Mobility manifesto*. Retrieved 28/10/2012, 2012, from http://www.suttontrust.com/research/the-mobility-manifesto/

Treiman, D. J. (1970). Industrialization and social stratification. *Sociological Inquiry, 40*(2), 207–234. doi: 10.1111/j.1475-682X.1970.tb01009.x

UUK. (2013). Patterns and trends in UK higher education. Available at http://www.universitiesuk.ac.uk/highereducation/Pages/PatternsAndTrendsInUKHigherEducation2013.aspx#.VlMK0z9_t8E

Willetts, D. (2010). *Statement on higher education and student funding*. Retrieved February 11, 2013, from www.gov.uk/government/speeches/statement-on-higher-education-funding-and-student-finance--2

Woodley, A. (2012). Wider and wider still? A historical look at open-ness of the Open University of the United Kingdom. In T. Hinton-Smith (Ed.), *Widening participation in higher education: Casting the net wide*. Basingstoke: Palgrave Macmillan.

Woodley, A., & Wilson, J. (2002). British higher education and its older clients. *Higher Education, 44*(3–4), 329–347. doi:10.1023/a:1019857315244.

CHAPTER 3

Language Issues Facing Non-Traditional Students: Some Problems and Solutions

Megan Bruce, Simon Rees, and Julie Wilson

LANGUAGE PROFILE: FOUNDATION CENTRE COHORT

As has been discussed in previous chapters, the Durham University Foundation Centre has an unusual cohort in terms of linguistic competence. Although many programmes in the sector focus exclusively on either home students (presumed native speakers or with native-like competence) or international students (typically around B2 on the Common European Framework of Reference for Languages), our department teaches native and non-native speakers (henceforth, NS and NNS respectively) alongside each other. For this to be successful, our International English Language Testing System (IELTS) entry requirement is fairly high within the sector: 6.0 with no element below 5.5 for most programmes and 6.5 with no element below 6.0 for Law, Medicine and Pharmacy.

Our remit is to widen participation in Higher Education (HE) and many of our NS students are local, mature learners. The other key NS demographic is conversion students: those who studied traditional qualifications successfully but then decided to pursue study in a different

M. Bruce (✉) • S. Rees • J. Wilson
Foundation Centre, University of Durham, Pelaw House, Leazes Road, Durham DH1 1TA, UK

discipline. NNS students are either EU or international (from a fees perspective) and come from a range of linguistic backgrounds. We have fairly large numbers of Chinese and Arabic speakers, as well as students from many other countries around the world.

CURRICULUM-BASED LANGUAGE SUPPORT

Language support for Foundation Centre students has changed and evolved over the last decade. Ten years ago, home students were given no language support whilst international students were provided with material in English for Academic Purposes (EAP) only as a fringe activity delivered outside the academic timetable. Over the last decade, however, EAP has been firmly embedded in the curriculum for all students through the development of a suite of Academic Practice modules which combines language with study skills support. Different versions of this module exist for students studying Arts and Humanities, Social Sciences, Science, Business, and Medicine. Only the Physical Sciences students do not take an Academic Practice module and they are instead given a series of EAP classes tailored to the specific needs of their progression route.

From 2007 to 2013 we also ran a one-year International Foundation Year qualification which had a slightly lower IELTS entry requirement and therefore a stronger emphasis on academic language development than our four-year direct progression programmes. This stand-alone qualification was phased out in 2012 when direct progression options were established for all departments at Durham University.

ADDITIONAL LANGUAGE SUPPORT

Alongside the curriculum-based language input through the Academic Practice modules, we also have a team of contract EAP staff who provide additional targeted language support to students where needed. All students are given a diagnostic writing task during their induction week to help us to identify immediately who would benefit from extra language support.

One particular initiative that has been successful is Language Lunches/ Writing Workshops. These are scheduled sessions, one lunchtime per week, when students can drop in to seek advice on a piece of written work from an EAP tutor. Students who are identified as needing support as an outcome of the writing diagnostic are required to attend these sessions for the first term. In addition, within the chemistry course, specific language-focussed activities have been embedded in order to provide opportunities for all students to improve their understanding of scientific language within the course context.

Overview of Specific Language Needs

During the past few years, staff in the Foundation Centre have developed a number of initiatives to help our students overcome specific language issues which have hindered their academic progress. Before we discuss these initiatives, it is important first to explore the different kinds of language problems which our students tend to face.

Lexis

All teachers have the task of inducting students into their community of practice. In these disciplinary communities, members help one another to establish knowledge and norms (November & Day, 2012; Wenger, 1998). It is widely acknowledged that helping students to acquire the vocabulary they will need both to study their subject and to write academic English in a more general sense is one of the first challenges that staff and new students have to face (Berkenkotter, Huckin, & Ackerman, 1991; Drury & Webb, 1991; Freedman, 1987; November & Day, 2012; Woodward-Kron, 2004).

Given the need for students to learn new vocabulary in order to become members of their community of practice, the next obvious question is what lexical items students need to learn. Nation (2001) divides vocabulary into three groups: high frequency words (covering about 80% of most texts), academic vocabulary (words which are most often found in academic writing and which comprise 8–10% of academic texts) and technical vocabulary which is dictated by the subject area and typically covers around 5% of academic texts (Hyland & Tse, 2007, p. 236).

Hyland and Tse outline that there is significant evidence to suggest that first-year students tend to find academic vocabulary harder to learn than technical vocabulary because it is less likely to be taught explicitly (Flowerdew, 1993) and the large number of academic words mean that each lexical item occurs relatively infrequently (Worthington & Nation,1996). Hyland and Tse also dispute Nation's categorisation of vocabulary into the above three sections. Their research shows that Nation's academic vocabulary is still discipline specific. For example, they show that "the word process is far more likely to be encountered as a noun by science and engineering students than by social scientists" (Hyland & Tse, 2007, p. 244). Drawing on Trimble's (1985) claim that "in different disciplinary environments words may have quite different meanings" (ibid., p. 247), Hyland and Tse conclude that they cannot "support the division between academic and technical vocabulary" (ibid., p. 249).

> Some students find the terminology of Higher Education (HE) to be so unfamiliar to them as to constitute a linguistic taboo. One student on a Science programme explained that, he found terms such as "introduction" or "paragraph" almost impossible to say out loud, because they were so far outside his life experience and comfort zone. When asked to use these terms in a tutorial he was unable to, and likened the situation to one of his tutors as going into a pub and being asked to carry out a conversation using very explicit swear words.

A well-known study in the area of academic vocabulary is Coxhead's compilation of an Academic Word List (AWL) (2000). This research has been the basis of several learner textbooks, such as Schmitt and Schmitt (2005). The AWL identified 570 word families which are frequently used in academic texts. The list was based on a corpus compiled by Coxhead which consisted of 3.5 million words of academic writing, from 414 academic texts written by more than 400 authors across 28 subject areas (Schmitt & Schmitt, 2005, p. vi). Despite their disagreement regarding the classification of vocabulary, both Coxhead (2000) and Hyland and Tse (2007, p. 251) agree that lexical items need to be learnt in context and this idea formed the basis of our FOCUS corpus project (an abbreviation of "FOundation CorpUS").

Within science education, it has long been recognised that the vocabulary of science poses significant challenges for students (Pozo & Lorenzo, 2009; Wellington & Osborne, 2001). This language may take the form of words that have a specific meaning in science such as "work" and "weight" that is distinct from their everyday use as well as entirely new terminology. A range of studies have investigated student understanding of scientific language (Gardner, 1972; Pickersgill & Lock, 1991; Johnstone & Selepeng, 2001; Mudraya, 2006; Rincke, 2011; Song & Carheden, 2014; Cassels & Johnstone, 1983) and highlighted a number of difficulties. This work has tended to focus on school age pupils and also students for whom English is not their first language. Cassels and Johnstone (1983), for example, found that a word in a scientific context was harder to understand than the same word in a non-scientific context. They also highlighted how a combination of words may result in an expression with a difficult meaning. For example, the word "external" with "TV aerial" is easy for pupils, but when "external" was linked with "skeleton", it was much more difficult. They argue that when moving to a scientific context the student is on less familiar ground where perhaps the interpretation of a whole new context was necessary to find a meaning for a word. Several authors (Johnstone & Selepeng, 2001; Mudraya, 2006) have reported incidences of students selecting the opposite meaning for a given term. Cassels and Johnstone (1983) discuss the role of the lecturer in seeking connections between new and existing vocabulary and the importance of linking new information to existing relevant concepts. Learning is also problematic if the lecturer assumes prior understanding of a term. Some of our students, for example, have recalled in research interviews the impact of such situations:

> *The lecturer kept on referring to snip genes. We did not understand the term and failed to follow the lecture. It was only after the lecture that I discovered it was an abbreviation SNP referring to a Single Nucleotide Polymorphism.*
>
> Conversely, the same students recall a contrasting experience:
>
> *The lecturer took time to explain the meaning of terms and how to break words down, for example, hypochromic, to determine their meaning. I found the module much more accessible and enjoyable and achieved well in the exams.*

Grammar

As our EAP tutors met with students at Language Lunches or one-to-one appointments, a concern became apparent amongst our home students: having had no formal language training in the past, they do not typically have the metalanguage to talk about the linguistic problems they encounter. As a result, it can be very difficult to address the language issues they face in academic study because all the traditional EAP materials are aimed at NNS who have acquired a vocabulary to talk about language points.

Joan Didion famously said "Grammar is a piano I play by ear" and this sums up the feeling of our NS students towards any overt teaching of language. They are proficient speakers of English (though their writing is often markedly less proficient) but, to follow the analogy, cannot read music. They cannot comfortably discuss how method sections of reports need to be written in the passive voice, or how it is important to use Standard English (SE) past participles in academic writing rather than the dialect variants. Our home students do not expect to encounter linguistic difficulty when they begin their programme of study and often have significant confidence issues where grammar and lexis are concerned. They are surprised, for example, that words that they already know such as "heat," "process" and "energy" also have specific academic meanings and they have difficulty learning new language information.

> One particular example of this is a local mature student who was generally performing well academically but who was making a consistent error in her writing. She was using a non-standard variant of the present perfect, for example, "I have ran", "She has ate" rather than the SE "I have run", "She has eaten". The student came to get help with her writing, had a chat with an EAP tutor and was given some gap filling activities on the present perfect to complete in order to consolidate the standard variant. After this meeting, the student missed class for a number of days and then booked an appointment to talk to the Learning and Teaching leader about withdrawing from the programme.
>
> The student had been completely overwhelmed by the use of the terminology "present perfect" which represented for her the tip of an iceberg of potentially unknown areas she would be required to study. She expected to learn new material about her degree subject, but had not anticipated needing to study language in a more formal capacity. She had contacted the only other person she knew who had completed a degree and asked them whether they had heard of the present perfect. Very defensively, she argued that if her friend had managed to get a degree without knowing that terminology, she should also be able to do so.
>
> Based on this encounter, and many others of a similar nature, we developed a range of Data Driven Learning (DDL) activities (Johns 1991) based on our FOCUS corpus to circumvent the need for use of meta-language in helping Foundation Centre students address their grammar issues.

In this situation, our international students have two distinct advantages over the home students. Firstly, because English is not their first language they expect to encounter linguistic difficulties and to have to work to solve them. Secondly, they have meta-language: because they are already language learners, they have the vocabulary to talk about their difficulties in order to receive support.

A key grammatical area that both NS and NNS tend to struggle with is the development of an appropriately formal academic voice. Swales and Feak (2004, pp. 22–23) list some common features of formal writing: avoiding contractions (e.g. "isn't", "don't"), using appropriate negative forms (e.g. "few" instead of "not many"), limiting the use of run on expressions (e.g. "and so forth"), avoiding addressing the reader as "you", avoiding direct questions, and placing adverbs within the verb (e.g. "the model was originally developed"). Sowton (2012, pp. 87–89) adds to this list: vague forms (e.g. "thing", "stuff"), slang terms (e.g. "kids"), phrasal verbs (e.g. "look up to" versus "admire"), idioms (e.g. "on the one hand…on the other hand"); clichés (e.g. "a level playing field", "back on track"). He also points out other common language errors such as fragment sentences, lack of subject–verb agreement and misplaced commas (Sowton, 2012, p. 197).

Discourse

The academic community of practice is further extended when considering the genres of writing that students are expected to read, understand and produce at university, and in the structuring of spoken activities such as seminars and presentations. Swales (1990) defined discourse communities as "groups that have goals or purposes, and use communication to achieve these goals." Within this academic discourse community, there are many sub-communities with a range of discipline-specific conventions. We have already established that the meaning of vocabulary may differ between disciplines, but students also need to understand that the forms of writing and speaking that they would use may be different.

Students gradually become familiar with the generic norms of academic writing and speaking over the course of their studies, but it is important that they also learn to recognise features of discourse that are common in their field of study. Research has been carried out to identify these differences; for example, genre analysts look for common "moves" and features in texts that share a communicative purpose. Swales (1990) developed this concept of rhetorical moves, and this has guided much of the teaching of EAP.

Many studies have been carried out in an attempt to enhance student learning in HE. One example of these is Phillip Nathan, a lecturer at Durham, who acknowledged some of the challenges faced by Business students. His paper investigates whether it is possible to identify moves in business case reports, thereby meaning that they are a text genre in themselves and can be recognised and taught as such. One of the main conclusions drawn from this investigation is that the findings support the idea of "specialism based pedagogy" (Nathan, 2013).

Due to the wide range of progression routes offered by the Foundation Centre, there is a need to prepare our student groups for both general academic skills and their chosen disciplines. Within Foundation Centre modules, corpus-based teaching activities are used to allow students to explore the use of language in different genres of texts produced by Durham University students. The corpus allows users to search by type of text (essay, lab report, dissertation, reflection, etc.) as well as by subject and level to uncover the different norms of these genres (http://community.dur.ac.uk/foundation.focus/).

Phonology

Phonology is defined as "the component of ... linguistic knowledge that is concerned with the physical realization of language" (Kenstowicz, 1994, p. 2). It is a fundamentally different language system from grammar: phonological knowledge is stored in the memory because the relation between sound and meaning is arbitrary and therefore, unpredictable. Teaching of this system includes pronunciation of sounds (both in isolation and connected speech), word stress, sentence stress/rhythm and intonation.

Phonology is the language system on which we focus least in our foundation modules, but there are some key aspects of support which are provided in this area. In the past, when a larger proportion of our students were international with a lower IELTS score, we used to run pronunciation workshops as part of an EAP module. These workshops would target students in three groups: those whose first language (L1) was Chinese, those whose L1 was Arabic and those whose L1 was something else. EAP modules taken exclusively by international students would use International Phonetic Alphabet (IPA) script for noting down new lexical items and would focus on activities such as stress patterning in connected speech. International induction activities often focused on intonation patterns in situations such as role plays of college life or meetings with tutors.

In the current cohort, our international students have a higher IELTS score and therefore, better pronunciation and phonological awareness. We also no longer have EAP modules dedicated to international students; instead they are mixed with native speakers and organised by the progression route. Nevertheless, we do include some phonological features in our teaching on various modules.

In our Academic Practice modules, all students complete both summative and formative oral presentations. In the classroom materials supporting presentation skills, we stress the importance of practising presentations aloud and considering intonation and connected speech features. In language support for Science students, we not only look at affixation in relation to common meanings but also in relation to stress shifts (e.g. photograph versus photographic). A dictionary skills session is taught to all students which focuses partly on the importance of correct pronunciation of new vocabulary items.

Overview of Language Support Initiatives

As is apparent from the above discussion, language support is a priority. To this end, staff have initiated a number of scholarship projects that focus on language support, and these will be outlined below.

Glossary

Our initial response to helping students with vocabulary issues was to develop a suite of activities (www.dur.ac.uk/foundation.science) including an online glossary to which students could contribute, and some online activities covering areas such as meanings of affixes to enable students to determine the meaning of unfamiliar words (Rees & Bruce, 2012). These continue to be used by students studying science subjects with some success. However, using these activities and other similar activities from the EAP Toolkit (http://www.elanguages.ac.uk/eap_toolkit.php) highlighted a concern amongst our home students that they do not have the metalanguage to talk about the problems they encounter with language and thus it can be very difficult to address the problem.

FOCUS *Corpus*

We decided that the best way to help our students learn the vocabulary they needed for their studies was to build a corpus of student texts which our students could then search using a concordancer. This decision was informed by the following:

- Our students did not have the knowledge to benefit from being explicitly taught about language and yet their written work contained significant errors;
- Words need to be "noticed" between 5 and 16 times in order to be learnt (Nation 1990);
- "Noticing" needs to take place in authentic contexts;
- DDL can allow individual learners to make their own discoveries about language.

Our project is entitled "FOCUS" which is an abbreviation of "FOundation CorpUS." It is a corpus of academic writings produced by Durham University students (undergraduate and postgraduate) in various (initially Science, Technology Engineering and Maths (STEM)) subjects. Tribble (1997) cautions against using apprentice performances as corpus data. However, we would argue that since the function of our corpus is to teach foundation students to write like conventional university students, in this case student writings are expert rather than apprentice performances.

Criteria for Text Inclusion

Acquiring texts to include in a project of this nature is always difficult as it requires the cooperation of a range of different people (Alsop & Nesi, 2009, pp. 76–81). Some of our texts are PhD theses which are freely accessible within the university. However, the majority of our texts have been sent to us by students for inclusion in the corpus. We have targeted one university department at a time, explained our project to them and asked for permission to contact their students and ask them to send us copies of strong examples of academic writing. We define "strong example" as a piece of work which was assessed at 60% or above by the department. With the help of each department, we identified particular assignments which exemplified a genre of academic writing in that subject area. We obtained a list of students who had scored 60% or more in that particular assignment and contacted them to ask them to send us a copy of their assignment. The contact email outlined the aims of and ethical procedures of the project. To incentivise students to send us their writing, we entered all names of contributors into a draw for a £100 Amazon voucher each term. So far we have successfully obtained texts from Chemistry, Earth Sciences, Physics, History, Sociology, Criminology, Sport and Business departments and are in the process of approaching more departments across the university. Our eventual aim is to include coverage from all departments.

Audio Feedback

Where possible, our tutors try to give written feedback on persistent language errors and the organisation of their writing to students on both formative and summative assessments; however, understandably many subject tutors with little experience in language teaching and EAP are reluctant to do this in great detail. Our language lunches and writing workshops have been reasonably effective, and we adapt these to the needs of the cohort of students. Unfortunately, despite this provision we have often observed little evidence of improvement, and we had growing concerns that some students were not fully engaging with this dialogue. In addition, some students indicated that they would appreciate more individual oral feedback sessions on assignments. Although we are happy to provide this where possible, it is often impractical to provide this level of individual support for every student. For this reason, we decided to review our own practice and look into alternative methods of providing feedback.

Looking at research into the provision of feedback, Race and Pickford (2007, p. 116) point out that feedback is increasingly an area of concern in the National Student Survey in the UK. Students want more detailed "forward-pointing" advice that helps them to improve their work, rather than tutors highlighting the negative aspects of their writing. Growing student numbers mean that the traditional method of providing primarily written feedback is perceived as less effective, and this has prompted much of the recent research. At the Foundation Centre, we are strongly motivated by the desire to improve student engagement with feedback, and we employ a range of methods to encourage students to use their feedback effectively.

Much of the research in this field is influenced by the constructivist argument; from this perspective, as knowledge and understanding are constructed by the way learners interact with the world, this is equally true about the way students learn from tutor feedback. Rather than simply transmitting feedback on errors to the student, Laurillard (2002, p. 55) indicates the need to "make the right connection between action and feedback," pointing out that feedback needs to be in the appropriate format to be understood, and that "it needs to be meaningful to be useful."

Over two decades ago, Ramsden (1992) introduced the idea that technology was bringing about change in university teaching. There is also now common agreement that we need to be aware of the needs of different types of learners, and therefore we should adapt our feedback accordingly. Brinko (1993, p. 583) suggests that, "feedback is more effective when it is sensitive to the recipient's locus of control," which suggests that our current dialogic method of feedback, where students are expected to engage with suggestions and work out the rephrasing themselves, is certainly appropriate for students with an internal locus of control, as they respond well to this type of self-discovery. However, others with an external locus of control may require more comprehensive and varied input. There is general agreement that feedback is most effective when provided using a variety of methods in a timely way, using specific language and phrasing; this initial research guided our decision to trial using recorded audio feedback in one specific essay assignment for our Business students. The essays were first marked and annotated, and the key points were explained in detail in MP3 file recordings and then used as an alternative method of providing feedback to students.

The results from our small trial certainly appear to support the use of technology to provide student feedback at the Foundation Centre, and this audio feedback was welcomed equally by home and international students. One interesting observation was the positive response from students receiving poor marks for the assignment: they felt that listening to the clearly explained constructive criticism, rather than simply reading "negative" comments, was seen as supportive rather than critical. From the tutor's perspective, it was rather satisfying to have the opportunity to expand on and explain the annotations made on the essay, and also easier to connect them to the assessment criteria. It was also easier to clarify language and phrasing errors, and avoided the risk of returning an essay overloaded with feedback that may also be difficult to read.

Conclusion

This chapter has reviewed the language issues typically faced by foundation students in the areas of lexis, grammar, discourse and phonology. It has proposed some solutions that we have implemented successfully with our non-traditional cohort, some of which continue to develop in different directions. The FOCUS corpus which was initially developed for use in foundation classes is now being used in other Durham departments as well as by other HEIs. We continue to explore solutions to the specific problems faced by a non-traditional cohort as successful academic study must always be underpinned by a comprehensive understanding of academic English.

References

Alsop, S., & Nesi, H. (2009). Issues in the development of the British Academic Written English (BAWE) corpus. *Corpora, 4*(1), 71–83.

Berkenkotter, C., Hukin, T., & Ackerman, J. (1991). Social context and socially constructed texts: The initiation of a graduate student into a writing research community. In C. Bazerman & J. Paradis (Eds.), *Textual dynamics of the professions* (pp. 191–215). Madison: The University of Wisconsin Press.

Brinko, K. T. (1993). The practice of giving feedback to improve teaching: What is effective? *The Journal of Higher Education, 64*(5), 574–593. JSTOR [Online] Available at: http://www.jstor.org/stable/2959994. Accessed 04 April 2013.

Cassels, J., & Johnstone, A. (1983). The meaning of words and the teaching of chemistry. *Education in Chemistry, 20*, 10–11.

Coxhead, A. (2000). A new academic word list. *TESOL Quarterly, 34*, 213–238.

Drury, H., & Webb, C. (1991). Literacy at tertiary level: Making explicit the writing requirements of a new culture. Paper presented at the *Inaugural Systematic Linguistics Conference*, Deakin University.

Flowerdew, J. (1993). Concordancing as a tool in course design. *System, 21*, 231–244.

Freedman, A. (1987). Learning to write again: Discipline specific writing at university. *Carleton Papers in Applied Language Studies, 4*, 45–65.

Gardner, R. P. L. (1972). *Words in science*. Victoria: Australian Science Education Project.

Hyland, K., & Tse, P. (2007). Is there an academic vocabulary? *TESOL Quarterly, 41*(2), 235–253.

Johns, T. F. (1991). Should you be persuaded: Two examples of data-driven learning. In T. F. Johns & P. King (Eds.), *Classroom concordancing* (pp. 1–13). Birmingham: ELR.

Johnstone, A. H., & Selepeng, D. (2001). A language problem revisited. *Chemistry Education: Research and Practice in Europe, 2*, 19–29.
Kenstowicz, M. (1994). *Phonology in generative grammar*. Oxford: Blackwell.
Laurillard, D. (2002). *Rethinking university teaching*. London: Routledge.
Mudraya, O. (2006). Engineering English: A lexical frequency instructional model. *English for Specific Purposes, 25*, 23–56.
Nathan, P. (2013). Academic writing in the business school: The genre of the business case report. *Journal of English for Academic Purposes, 12*(1), 57–68. Available at http://www.sciencedirect.com/science/article/pii/S1475158512000768. Accessed 01 September 2014.
Nation, I. S. P. (1990). *Teaching and Learning Vocabulary*. Boston: Heinle & Heinle.
Nation, I. S. P. (2001). *Learning vocabulary in another language*. New York: CUP.
November, N., & Day, K. (2012). Using undergraduates' digital literacy skills to improve their discipline-specific writing: A dialogue. *International Journal for the Scholarship of Learning and Teaching, 6*(2), 1–21.
Pickersgill, S., & Lock, R. (1991). Student understanding of selected non-technical words in science. *Research in Science & Technological Education, 9*, 71–79.
Pozo, J., & Lorenzo, M. (2009). Representing organic molecules: The use of chemical languages by university students. In C. Andersen, N. Scheuer, M. P. Perez Echeverria, & T. Ev (Eds.), *Representational systems and practices as learning tools*. Rotterdam: Sense Publishers.
Race, P., & Pickford, R. (2007). *Making teaching work*. London: Sage.
Ramsden, P. (1992). *Learning to teach in higher education*. London: Routledge.
Rees, S. W., & Bruce, M. (2012). The development of online resources to enhance understanding of subject specific language in non-traditional students. *12th Annual Durham Blackboard Users' Conference*, Durham University, January 2012.
Rincke, K. (2011). It's rather like learning a language: Development of talk and conceptual understanding in mechanics lessons. *International Journal of Science Education, 33*, 229–258.
Schmitt, D., & Schmitt, N. (2005). *Focus on vocabulary: Mastering the academic word list*. London: Longman.
Song, Y., & Carheden, S. (2014). Dual meaning vocabulary words (DMW) in learning chemistry. *Chemistry Education Research and Practice, 15*, 128–141.
Sowton, C. (2012). *50 steps to improving your academic writing*. Reading: Garnet Education.
Swales, J. M. (1990). *Genre analysis: English in academic and research settings*. Cambridge: Cambridge University Press.
Swales, J. M., & Feak, C. B. (2004). *Academic writing for graduate students* (2nd ed.). Ann Arbor: University of Michigan Press.

Tribble, C. (1997). Improvising corpora for ELT: Quick-and-dirty ways of developing corpora for language teaching. In J. Melia & B. Lewandowska-Tomaszczyk (Eds.), *PALC 1997 proceedings*. Lodz: Lodz University Press. Retrieved from http://www.ctribble.co.uk/text/Palc.htm. Accessed 5 February 2013.

Trimble, L. (1985). *English for science and technology: A discourse approach*. Cambridge: Cambridge University Press.

Wellington, J. J., & Osborne, J. (2001). *Language and literacy in science education*. Buckingham: Open University Press.

Wenger, E. C. (1998). *Communities of practice: Learning, meaning and identity*. New York/Cambridge: Cambridge University Press.

Woodward-Kron, R. (2004). Discourse communities and writing apprenticeship: An investigation of these concepts in undergraduate education students' writing. *Journal of English for Academic Purposes, 3*, 139–161.

Worthington, D., & Nation, I. S. P. (1996). Using texts to sequence the introduction of new vocabulary in an EAP course. *RELC Journal, 27*(2), 1–11.

CHAPTER 4

Teaching Mathematics to Adults: Integrating New and Old Knowledge

Mary Dodd, Jean Mathias, and Sam J. Nolan

MATHEMATICS PROFILE: FOUNDATION CENTRE COHORT

Mature students in the Foundation Centre need to develop mathematics at different levels and for a range of applications according to their future study direction. Required outcomes may vary from higher level mathematical concepts and algorithms for physics and engineering, to manipulation of number and proportional reasoning for pharmacy or statistics for research across a variety of academic disciplines. Developing an appropriate pedagogy requires not only an understanding of the general issues involved in teaching mathematical concepts to any student but also an awareness of the additional issues that adult students, in particular, may face.

In his discussion on andragogy, Knowles (1980, p. 45) suggests that adults are self-directed learners who bring with them a "reservoir of experience that becomes an increasingly rich resource for learning." The discussion that follows considers the implications of these two ideas for

---

M. Dodd (✉) • J. Mathias
Foundation Centre, University of Durham, Pelaw House, Leazes Road, Durham DH1 1TA, UK

S.J. Nolan
Centre for Academic, Researcher and Organisation Development,
Durham University, Durham DH1 3LE, UK

© The Editor(s) (if applicable) and The Author(s) 2016
C.A. Marshall et al. (eds.), *Widening Participation, Higher Education and Non-Traditional Students*,
DOI 10.1057/978-1-349-94969-4_4

foundation teaching and the difficulties associated with their interaction. It is followed by two snapshots of practice that highlight how these ideas affect our approach.

- The first considers how the requirement of mental mathematics for professional practice in fields such as Pharmacy and Primary Education can be used as a catalyst to develop new ways of teaching and challenge the notion of the "one best method."
- The second considers how misconceptions in Newtonian mechanics based on life experience and previous teaching can be identified and overcome through the introduction of dialogue-driven interactive classroom environments.

Both examples highlight the benefit of making processes and choices explicit to students, facilitating the integration of previous understanding with new ways of working without disempowerment and increasing the potential for new learning to be built.

Engaging with Foundation Students as Self-directed Learners

Observations of adult foundation students, suggest that Knowles's (1980) description of adults as self-directed is very appropriate if adults are considered at a meta level, rather than in individual learning situations. In a teaching session, adults frequently expect to be teacher-led, but take control of their own learning and engage with the process because they want to be there (Duffin & Simpson, 2000). They motivate themselves to study outside the classroom and beyond the topic and are proactive in seeking help. Further, and perhaps increasingly in the current climate, adults have a clear expectation of what the teacher-led process should be and this is often strongly related to their views of teaching from their past, even if previous experiences have not been positive (Duffin & Simpson, 2000).

Adults also have an expectation of what mathematics itself should be and which aspects are of most value, again often related to past teaching. The debate about the use or not of calculators is an example of this. Schoenfeld (1992) noted that typical student beliefs include the notion that there is one right answer obtained by one right method and that every problem should be answered in less than five minutes. Coben (2000) argued that this notion of one right method is widely held amongst adults.

She suggested people believe that each operation has only one standard algorithm that can be used to solve it and, further, that this is usually the algorithm that has been taught in school.

Knowles's (1980) second observation about previous knowledge appears to make a value judgement about the students' previous experience. The adjective "rich" implies that the experience is always a positive resource but Schoenfeld (1992), for example, noted that a knowledge base can also contain misconceptions, misremembered facts and other things which are untrue and Karsenty (2002), and Duffin and Simpson (2000) have highlighted issues with accuracy of reconstructed knowledge. Further, the belief in this knowledge based on experience of apparent success in the past, may make these ideas harder to change (Skemp, 1979). Associative strength of mathematical facts, confidence in answers and remembered algorithms are all linked to previous experience and may all be instrumental in strategy selection in the future. Further, the accumulated "reservoir of experience" (Knowles, 1980, p. 45) contains not just the mathematics itself but also the so-called affective processes, belief, attitudes and emotion, towards that mathematics (See Chap. 10). The passage of time and influence of home, work and adult life in general result in a very different starting point for adults compared with children.

Using a constructivist approach, people build their new learning on previous learning. However, the previous discussion suggests that some previous knowledge will be incorrect, confused or holds back new construction.

Dodd takes constructivism further and considers learning through the metaphor of building on a Greenfield or Brownfield site and this underpins all mathematics teaching at the centre (2008, 2012). On a Greenfield site, a builder can build a series of new houses to a standard design from foundation to roof. Completing a partially built house on such a site at a later date simply requires slotting into the correct stage of the building process. Thus, beyond assumptions of basic skills such as addition and multiplication, the teacher attempts to build a new set of learning by either ignoring anything already there or assuming that what is there is the same as their design and can be built on or linked to.

If there was just one possible order or hierarchy in which mathematics could be taught, one method and one absolute understanding, adult tutors would effectively be rebuilding the same building that had been built in school. Re-teaching would fill in the missing gaps, consolidate and reaffirm what has been remembered correctly and replace incorrect reconstructions with new correct information. This "start again and fill in the gaps" approach is the underlying principle behind the design of many "adult returner" resources.

However, there is not just one possible hierarchy. Gagné (1968, p. 3) noted "Do they represent a sole learning route to the learning of the final task, or perhaps even a most efficient route? ... It is quite apparent that the answer is no." An adult may have developed a set of alternative sub-skills through home and work. Starting again and filling the gaps fails to make use of this "rich resource for learning" (Knowles, 1980, p. 45) and denies opportunities for consolidation and empowerment. A more major problem occurs if the new building bears little relation to the old building at all (at least according to student perceptions). Knowledge built elsewhere, whether correct or flawed, whether potentially useful or not, might exist in a parallel storage system where it might or might not re-emerge in some alternative context.

A further problem with "starting again" occurs if transformation of learning has taken place. In some learning, lower levels of learning simply act as prerequisites for the next level (Gagné, 1985); so for example, working on questions like $3x + 2 = 2x - 5$ consolidates the skills required to solve simpler problems, such as $3x = 12$. However, if a lower level undergoes transformation and is subsumed to form a higher one, it is not possible to go back to the previous level. This distinction between consolidation and transformation between levels is an important one for considering teaching approaches for adults. If consolidation occurs by revisiting earlier work, "starting from the beginning" seems a possible strategy. However, if earlier work has been transformed and absorbed (accommodation), revisiting that earlier work may not be constructive or desirable. Indeed, Meyer and Land's work on threshold concepts which exist within every curriculum goes further (Meyer & Land, 2003). Mastering threshold concepts has a powerful and transformative effect on the learner, changing their internal view, so much so that moving back to an earlier method of thinking is not possible.

The notion of leaving past educational experiences behind and making a new start is a popular and comforting one for some adult returners, particularly those with high anxiety levels and little confidence in their previous learning. However, as Evans (2000) states, this is clearly a fantasy. Starting from the beginning and covering work that children would cover in school in less than a year, inevitably leads to narrower teaching and a very behaviourist approach. One method is taught, which may or may not link with adult memories, rather than an exploration of alternative methods. Teaching is based on the development of one hierarchy of sub-skills selected by the tutor rather than a consideration of multiple alternative hierarchies (Gagné, 1968, 1969, 1985). If a student truly began again and made no links with anything previously learnt, the resulting workload would be immense.

Sometimes, students who have managed in the past might be reluctant to revisit or unpick what they might perceive as fragile learning. For them the notion of "filling in the gaps" or the remedial approach might be more attractive. However, this is essentially built on the same behaviourist model as the "new start" and relies on a belief in one right method or one hierarchy of learning. Increasingly popular in university pre-arrival courses, where there is a growing awareness of issues around larger student cohorts and perceived deficits in existing knowledge, the purpose is usually to ensure everyone is ready for the next stage with little recognition that multiple methods and understanding may exist.

Whilst such pre-arrival courses acknowledge that some knowledge is already there and can confer a level of autonomy to learners to identify their own gaps, they fail to recognise the dangers of incomplete or partial knowledge. Nor do they recognise that some knowledge may be incorrect or have been corrupted or distorted by experiences. Misunderstandings and particularly overgeneralisations, can slip through the net unchallenged and provide a restrictive influence on future learning. Further, evidence from Dodd (2012) indicates that "correct answers" may not always indicate competence in the specific set of sub-skills envisaged by an educator. Adults sometimes use a range of alternative strategies, such as intuitive responses, which are a function of number (non-conservation of operation [Greer, 1994]), common sense mathematics (Coben, 2000) and trial and error to select answers, using their greater recognition of reasonableness (Benn, 1997).

Returning to the metaphor of a Brownfield site, the builder needs first to survey existing structures to identify what could be built on or incorporated into a new design. They would, then decide how one structure might be reliant on another, and focus particularly on what is unsafe or should be demolished (Dodd, 2012). Using this metaphor highlights the importance of identifying and confronting incorrect and confused knowledge if a new stronger construction is to be built.

These notions of adapting teaching through identifying existing knowledge are prevalent in all mathematics teaching at the Centre and are drawn out further in the following case studies.

Case Study 1: A New Approach to Teaching "Mental Mathematics"

Challenging the Notion of "One Right Method" and Identifying the Role of Number in Method Selection

The use, overuse and misuse of calculators can be the subject of debate. The recognition that there is a need for non-calculator mathematics skills was reflected in the inclusion of non-calculator papers within Mathematics General Certificate of Secondary Education (GCSE) exams and "mental mathematics" sections within Key Stage 2 and 3 testing. In some professions, particularly for teachers and pharmacists, there is a clear recognition of the need for non-calculator and/or mental mathematics skills and, hence, students need to pass appropriate proficiency tests before being allowed to practise. This has resulted in a proliferation of books and websites intended to support preparation for such tests. Some resources are more helpful than others but, sadly, some may actually be detrimental to the development of appropriate skills. Further, the need for proficiency goes beyond the notion of the test as simply a gatekeeping exercise to a recognition that such skills may be vital within the classroom or essential in life's critical decisions.

We have been trialling a new approach designed to overcome some of the underlying issues which may prevent understanding or use of methods and build a framework which helps alternative methods to be stored and retrieved. Additionally, this approach encourages a more critical evaluation of the available resources allowing students to gain maximum benefit from independent reading and practice. The teaching process involves making explicit some of the differences between formal and informal methods, particularly the influence of number on method selection. This is linked with an attempt to identify and challenge hidden beliefs in the "one right method." To explain the rationale for this approach and why it is deemed of value, it is helpful to first visit some of the underlying theory and evidence.

Mathematics is practised in different ways by different people in different situations. Whilst there is no clear separation, the term "informal methods" tends to refer to those which are often practised outside the classroom and without the use of calculators. A well known example of this is the method used by Brazilian street vendors for finding the price of 10 coconuts by adding three lots of three and one more (Carraher,

Carraher, & Schliemann, 1985). Indeed, a number of informal methods involve the use of building and adding. Formal methods tend to refer to the use of algorithmic procedures which may involve the use of pen and paper and are more likely to benefit from the use of a calculator.

This difference can be illustrated using the example of finding 6% of 840. Formal methods are likely to involve a multiplication of 6 and 840 and a division by 100 (or a multiplication of 840 by 0.06). An informal build and add method might involve the finding of 10% (84), then 5% (42) then 1% (8.4) and adding the 5% and 1% values. However, this is only one of many possible informal methods. An alternative example of finding 23% of 400 might be more efficiently solved by the recognition that 23% of 100 is 23, 23% of 200 is 46 and 23% of 400 is 92 but this method would not readily translate to the finding of 23% of 730. The selection of the most efficient informal method is, therefore, related to the numbers within the problem (non-conservation of operation [Greer, 1994]) whereas the use of a formal method is independent of number.

During a pilot study, when 203 students were asked to find 6% of 250 at the beginning of their course without using a calculator, most selected an informal method. When the same question was given to the same students part of the way through the course, most had changed to a formal method.

Formal methods may well have been used more recently and, therefore, are more likely to be the first methods to be remembered. However, this is not sufficient to explain why some people wrote down a formal calculation which they could not calculate without a calculator, even though they had successfully obtained an answer in the previous questionnaire using informal methods. It is possible that the informal method had been forgotten but interviews with students (Dodd, 2012) suggested that some people felt informal methods were not legitimate in academic situations, an issue also identified by Duffin and Simpson (2000).

The distinction between a method that appears to work whatever the numbers and methods that are limited by the numbers within the question helps explain why more formal methods might be actively encouraged and, indeed, become essential in the sciences where real experimental data is unlikely to lend itself to informal methods of calculation. Alatorre and Figueras (2005) noted how adults used a variety of methods to answer proportional reasoning questions but that the most highly qualified of the scientists in the group always used the same formal method, arguing that it was the only method that was infallible. However, there is a difference between recognising that one method is superior to another in certain types of problems and deciding that this method is always superior. Those that fail to recognise this difference may take the "non-calculator" instruction to mean that the same formal method must be used resulting in a time-consuming pen and paper algorithm, often long multiplication or division. Those that do recognise the difference, will look for a more efficient method using the numbers given or, perhaps, by estimating.

One further issue needs to be explored. Schoenfeld (1992) argued that people often expect one right answer to a mathematics problem. Coben (2000) went further and argued that some adults also expect one right method. She suggested people believe that each operation has only one standard algorithm that can be used to solve it and, further, that this is usually the algorithm that has been taught in school. Through informal discussions with students (Dodd, 2012) it appeared that even if the notion of one right method was not held, the notion of the one best method often was.

One student recalled a session on percentages where a number of alternative methods had been introduced. She recognised that a number of different methods existed but in the end decided to stick with the method that worked for her and let the tutor stick to the method that the tutor liked.

> I think that's what she had been taught at school that worked for her so she stuck with it just like I stuck with mine.

and later:

> So if we were doing percentages, she would use her method that she was more comfortable with, I think it was just to find a method that we could all do and we each could find a method that worked for us rather than just one way of thinking.
> (Dodd, 2012, p. 208)

As Lithner (2008) noted, people are often prepared to stay with something that appears to give a satisfactory answer rather than searching for something deeper. There may also be a concern about destabilising or confusing existing understanding by considering other ways of working. The need to prepare for skills tests and complete questions as fast and efficiently as possible provides a legitimate reason for people to have to explore alternative methods, even if this risks a temporary disequilibrium. Thus, the existence of such tests acts as a catalyst for increasing people's flexibility of approach, a valuable prerequisite for gaining deeper understanding of mathematics.

Making explicit the distinction between formal and informal methods and their interaction with number, and explaining why people may be less familiar with some methods, provides both an introduction and structure for new learning. Perhaps equally valuably, it provides a new start, a new approach and removes the remedial feel of some "mental mathematics" teaching and resources. Many of those attending the sessions have already attempted mock or diagnostic tests and begin with a sense of failure. Informal feedback from these students and the return of students the following week if sessions are voluntary, suggests that this is something of a "light bulb" session for some people. A further consequence is the acceptance and willingness to explore and explain each other's methods so that valuable learning can take place simply by asking a few timed mental mathematics questions and then comparing and debating. This openness and interest in the solutions of others has led to a new dynamic within the student cohort so that students are far more frequently observed to be scaffolding each other than has been observed in the past.

Case Study 2: A New Approach to Mechanics

Teaching Mechanics by Identifying and Confronting Threshold Concepts

The applied mathematics subject of mechanics has been noted for many years to be particularly difficult to teach effectively (e.g. Gilbert, 1982, p. 62). Much work has been done focussed on common misconceptions that students bring with them from their previous education and common everyday experience, the "brown" material in our Brownfield site analogy. A simple example of a common misconception relates to the work of Galileo in showing that objects of differing mass fall at the same rate. When asked "if I drop a tonne of bricks and a tonne of feathers from the same height, ignoring air resistance which hits the grounds first?," many students opt for the bricks, whereas, of course, the answer is that both hit the ground simultaneously. The greater their life experience, the more embedded the misconception; so for more mature students, mechanics is particularly challenging.

Elements of mechanics have long been identified as threshold concepts discussed earlier (Meyer & Land, 2003). Engaging with threshold concepts is also likely to be troublesome for the student. They are often characterised by super complexity or perhaps troublesome because "the learner remains 'defended' and does not wish to change or let go of their customary way of seeing things" (Perkins, 2006; Land, Cousin, Meyer, & Davies, 2005, Land, Meyer, & Baillie, 2010). As Meyer and Land (2003) note, "difficulty in understanding threshold concepts may leave the learner in a state of liminality."

To understand misconceptions among our mature students, a diagnostic test was used before and after teaching. The Force Concept Inventory (FCI) is a diagnostic test composed of 30 questions that grew out of research carried out by Hestenes, Wells, and Swackhamer (1992) in the USA. The questions are targeted at 28 common misconceptions which are grouped into six categories: kinematics, impetus, active force, action–reaction pairs, concatenation of influences and other influences on motion.

Interviews in conjunction with the diagnostic test reveal that mature students have misconceptions in all areas of Newton's laws. The mean FCI test score before teaching was about 40%, similar to scores seen for those unfamiliar with Newton's laws in previous studies (e.g. Hake, 1998). These misconceptions are not related to other mathematical skills, for example, algebra, but are rather a function of the student's ability to model the situation presented. Common misconceptions based on "common sense" play a role here and examples are discussed below:

Misconception 1

Students have trouble imagining how an object can move in the absence of an external force. During conversations about Newton's law, it is noticed that students also often mix up "force" and "velocity," when they speak about "force" they actually mean velocity. They often "see" velocity as a force.

Misconception 2

Students struggle to distinguish the relationships between force, acceleration and velocity. They often think force causes velocity, because they can easily experience force and velocity in daily life, but not acceleration. Often students have difficulty understanding a concept when they cannot imagine it happening in real life. Typical student comments include:

If you put a certain amount of force into a system, then there is a certain amount of velocity coming out but it would be impossible to increase it continuously.

In reality, you don't think someone pushes a box, and the box continuously increases speed.

Misconception 3

Students have trouble differentiating Newton's Third Law from his Second Law when solving a real problem, because it is often difficult to see an action and equal reaction force in real life. Another student noted:

If a man pushes a car in order for it to move, he should push harder at the car to overcome the force that the car pushes back. Hence, the force that the man pushes the car with should be bigger than the force that the car pushes back at the man.

Teaching Practice to Improve Students' Newtonian Way of Thinking

To help students to understand these misconceptions we radically changed our teaching approach by making an active intervention to "force" students to challenge their intuitive thinking. Meyer and Land (2005) suggest that the crossing of a threshold will incorporate an enhanced and extended use of language, so our process included class discussions around students' common misconceptions.

To aid in this activity, purposefully designed multiple choice questions were used in class to expose students' misconceptions. Students were encouraged to use subject vocabulary and also reflect on their misunderstanding. For example, multiple choice questions on Newton's first law of motion were discussed in class, as shown below:

(1) An object following a straight line path at constant speed:

has zero acceleration
has no force acting on it
has a net force acting on it in the direction of motion
must be moving in a vacuum
none of these.

(2) A person walking on a level surface moves forward because of the force of:

the feet pushing down on the ground
the feet pushing backwards on the ground
the ground pushing forwards on the feet
the ground pushing backwards on the feet
the willpower as a human being.

Students typically held heated discussion on the solutions to the questions above. In the first question, discussion focussed particularly around whether it matters if there is a force on the object. In the second question, students generally held the misconception that it is not possible for the ground to push forwards, and through discussion they came to understand the application of Newton's third law in this situation. These discussions were often accompanied by dramatic tutor-led demonstrations to aid students' comprehension and retention.

Measures of Success

The FCI was deployed pre and post teaching. These were compared using the class averaged normalised gain in the FCI test scores, given by the formula:

$$g = \frac{\%G}{\%G_{max}} = \frac{\%S_f - \%S_i}{100 - \%S_i}$$

Here, average normalised gain <g> for a course is the ratio of the actual average gain <G> to the maximum possible average gain <G_{Max}>, where <S_f> and <S_i> are the final (post) and initial (pre) class averages. In a seminal paper which had a significant impact on curricula in the USA, Hake (1998) compared the average normalised gain for 6542 students learning mechanics at a variety of levels [high school (HS), college (COLL) and university (UNIV)] and with two distinct teaching styles, traditional (e.g. transmissive styles) and interactive engagement, which was "designed at least in part to promote conceptual understanding through interactive engagement of students in heads-on (always) and hands-on (usually) activities which yield immediate feedback through discussion with peers and/or instructors" (Hake 1998, p. 65).

Hake showed that through the use of interactive engagement teachers could improve student performance typically with <g> values of 40% for those scoring 40% on the pre-test. Although we have a rather limited sample size, with a large spread, taken at face value, a gain in understanding (as measured by FCI score) amongst our local mature students is seen, which is in excess of any group monitored in the large statistical study of Hake. However, it should be noted that in Hake's earlier largescale study, the largest difference in gain seen was between groups M-PD95a-C (<g>=0.47) and M-PD95b-C (<g>=0.64). These were two cohorts of students who were taught with identical materials, but group M-PD95a-C were traditional "day" students at a college, whereas M-PD95b-C were "night-class" students, who were typically 7–10 years older than the day students, and as Hake (1998, p. 67) notes "were more mature and dedicated, possibly through paying their own way through school." Although the gain seen is not as pronounced as in this study, the motivation and resilience of mature students is seen as a factor in their enhanced gain.

Although the approach identified seems to reap very positive results, it should be noted that all students still have issues in applying Newton's Laws and that some misconceptions are more difficult to overcome than others. We will work to refine our methodology to address these remaining misconceptions in future studies.

Overview of Case Studies

Despite their surface differences, the two case studies selected here use a similar underlying process. Stage One involves the teacher's awareness of the likely existence of a common misconception within the group. Stage Two requires questions to be set to help make these misconceptions explicit to both the teacher and the student. Stage Three requires the teacher to provide an impetus for change which must be perceived by the student to be of sufficient value to override the fear of destabilising existing knowledge or skills. Finally, peer negotiation and interaction facilitated by the teacher scaffolds students to a new understanding.

The series of processes illustrated here is not unique to these selected case studies but can also be found in a variety of other mathematics learning events taking place in the Centre with similar success. However, it is important to highlight the importance of providing sufficient impetus for change. Without this, students will be unlikely to abandon current ways of thinking. Indeed, revisiting old knowledge carries the risk of strengthening and embedding it further. It is also essential that misconceptions are shared by a number of students within the group. Identifying that others share a view reduces feelings of shame and allows people to move forward without loss of empowerment. However, highlighting that an individual misconception is not shared by others can have the reverse effect. (see Chap. 10 for further discussion). Thus, the case studies used here can only represent one of the many strategies required for the successful development of mature mathematics learners, each of whom is unique.

Conclusion

This chapter presented the view that successful construction of new mathematics knowledge requires the interaction of new and old knowledge and, further, that old knowledge for mature students may be flawed and strongly embedded. Using the analogy of building on a Brownfield site, it was suggested that underlying knowledge and belief structures need to be explored and then demolished, updated or incorporated into any new learning to produce strongly built foundations unique to each student. Failure to recognise the nature of the ground and simply "start from the beginning", risks the creation of unstable structures which will exert a detrimental effect on future progress.

The two case studies selected in this chapter helped illustrate some of the mechanisms used by the Foundation Centre to enable people to self-identify areas where they hold specific misconceptions or non-optimal ways of working and to reach new understanding through negotiation and scaffolding. Our overall philosophy is to recognise each student as an individual learner with a unique knowledge base and to incorporate this recognition into all our teaching processes. By fully accepting the prior knowledge and experience our students bring with them, we are in a position to both support them on their educational journey and to allow them to see learning as a transformative and collaborative endeavour.

REFERENCES

Altorre, S., & Figueras, O. (2005). Proportional reasoning of adults with different levels of literacy. In M. Horne & B. Marr (Eds.), *Connecting voices in adult mathematics and numeracy: practitioners, researchers and learners*. Proceedings of the 12th international conference of Adults Learning Maths—A research forum, Melbourne, 42–47.

Benn, R. (1997). *Adults count too: Mathematics for empowerment*. Leicester: NIACE.

Carraher, T., Carraher, D., & Schliemann, A. (1985). Mathematics in the streets and in schools. *British Journal of Developmental Psychology, 3*, 21–29.

Coben, D. (2000). Mathematics or common sense? Researching 'invisible' mathematics through adults' life histories. In D. Coben, J. O'donoghue, & G. Fitzsimons (Eds.), *Perspectives on adults learning mathematics: Research and practice*. Dordrecht/Boston/London: Kluwer.

Dodd, M. (2008). CURRENT REPORT: The mathematical competence of adults returning to learning on a university foundation programme: a selective comparison of performance with the CSMS study. In E. Nardi, T. Rowland, & L. Haggarty (Eds.), *Research in mathematics education* (Vol. 10, pp. 203–204). Oxford: Routledge.

Dodd, M. (2012). *The influence of previous understanding and relative confidence on adult maths learning: Building adult understanding on a brownfield site.* Doctorate in Education thesis, Open University.

Duffin, J., & Simpson, A. (2000). Understanding their thinking: The tension between the cognitive and the affective. In D. Coben, J. O'donoghue, & G. Fitzsimons (Eds.), *Perspectives on adults learning mathematics research and practice*. Dordrecht/Boston/London: Kluwer.

Evans, J. (2000). *Adults' mathematical thinking and emotions: A study of numerate practice*. London/New York: Routledge Falmer.

Gagné, R. (1968). Presidential address of division 15 learning hierarchies. *Educational Psychologist, 6*(1), 1–9.

Gagné, R. (1969). *The conditions of learning*. London/New York/Sidney/Toronto: Holt, Rinehart and Winston.

Gagné, R. (1985). *The conditions of learning and theory of instruction* (4th ed.). New York: Rinehart and Winston.

Gilbert, J. K. (1982). Students' conceptions of ideas in mechanics. *Physics Education, 17*(2), 62–66.

Greer, B. (1994). Extending the meaning of multiplication and division. In G. Harel & J. Confrey (Eds.), *The development of multiplicative reasoning in the learning of mathematics*. Albany: State University of New York Press.

Hake, R. R. (1998). Interactive-engagement versus traditional methods: A six-thousand-student survey of mechanics test data for introductory physics courses. *American Journal of Physics, 66,* 64.

Hestenes, D., Wells, M., & Swackhamer, G. (1992). Force concept inventory. *The Physics Teacher, 30,* 141–158.

Karsenty, R. (2002). What do adults remember from their high school mathematics? The case of linear functions. *Educational Studies in Mathematics, 51,* 117–144.

Knowles, M. (1980). *The modern practice of adult education: From pedagogy to andragogy* (2nd ed.). New York: Cambridge University Press.

Land, R., Cousin, G., Meyer, J. H. F., & Davies, P. (2005). Threshold concepts and troublesome knowledge (3): Implications for course design and evaluation. In C. Rust (Ed.), *Improving student learning: Diversity and inclusivity, proceedings of the 12th improving student learning conference* (pp. 53–64). Oxford: Oxford Centre for Staff and Learning Development (OCSLD).

Land, R., Meyer, J. H. F., & Baillie, C. (2010). *Threshold concepts and transformational learning.* Rotterdam: Sense.

Lithner, J. (2008). A research framework for creative and imitative reasoning. *Educational Studies in Mathematics, 67,* 255–276.

Meyer, J. H. F., & Land, R. (2003). Threshold concepts and troublesome knowledge 1: Linkages to ways of thinking and practising. In C. Rust (Ed.), *Improving student learning: Theory and practice ten years on* (pp. 412–424). Oxford: Oxford Centre for Staff and Learning Development (OCSLD).

Meyer, J. H. F., & Land, R. (2005). Threshold concepts and troublesome knowledge (2): Epistemological considerations and a conceptual framework for teaching and learning. *Higher Education, 49*(3), 373–388.

Perkins, D. (2006). Constructivism and troublesome knowledge. In R. Land & J. H. F. Meyer (Eds.), *Overcoming barriers to student understanding: Threshold concepts and troublesome knowledge* (pp. 33–47). London/New York: Routledge/Taylor & Francis Group.

Schoenfeld, A. (1992). Learning to think mathematically: Problem solving, metacognition, and sense-making in mathematics. In D. Grouws (Ed.), *Handbook for research on mathematics teaching and learning* (pp. 334–370). New York: Macmillan.

Skemp, R. (1979). *The psychology of learning mathematics.* Middlesex: Pelican Books.

CHAPTER 5

Breaking Barriers: Overcoming Anxieties in Practical Science

Sam J. Nolan, Simon Rees, and Carole Rushall

In preparing students for science study, one key component is their ability to undertake laboratory study. Many universities have a strong focus on research-led education, and during the early years of any science degree programme, the focus is on the development of the key practical science skills necessary for deeper study in research projects in later years. To prepare them for undergraduate study, foundation students should be well versed in working within a laboratory environment or in the field, and in the core ideas of scientific investigation.

In focus groups with foundation students, we identified that although our expectation was that international students would have a relatively recent experience of learning laboratory-based science, this was often not the case. As in the UK, many countries focus on the theoretical when teaching science at Quality Assurance Agency for Higher Education (QAA) Level 3 equivalent. Mature, home students also tend to have had

---

S.J. Nolan (✉)
Centre for Academic, Researcher and Organisation Development, Durham University, Durham DH1 3LE, UK

S. Rees • C. Rushall
Foundation Centre, University of Durham, Pelaw House, Leazes Road, Durham DH1 1TA, UK

© The Editor(s) (if applicable) and The Author(s) 2016
C.A. Marshall et al. (eds.), *Widening Participation, Higher Education and Non-Traditional Students*,
DOI 10.1057/978-1-349-94969-4_5

little recent experience of practical laboratory learning. For both groups, this lack of experience can lead to an increased anxiety about the practical aspects of laboratory learning. In this chapter, we will introduce two key areas that we have identified as particular barriers to student learning: preparation and visualisation.

Barrier 1: Preparing for Practical Science

When conducting experiments in the laboratory, students are often concerned with the technical aspects of the experiments they are undertaking, whilst not considering the deeper underlying scientific mechanisms involved. These surface learning approaches, were clearly identified amongst students taking classes in Chemistry and Physics, but was also apparent amongst students in introductory classes in Earth Science, where a significant component of their assessment was focussed on their work in field trips. In their work on the development of scientific reasoning, based on prolonged observations of students engaged in laboratory learning, Kind and Osborne (in press) have identified this as an issue. They see conducting science as a three-stage process, namely:

Stage 1: Investigation

Investigation is the most obvious phase of scientific enquiry. Here students are interacting with the real world, making measurements and observations. For physical scientists, these are usually conducted in the laboratory, whereas for Earth scientists these also occur in the field.

Stage 2: Evaluation

At the core of scientific reasoning is the ability students have to question both primary and secondary sources of data and develop questions which link theory to experimental investigation. One often thinks of traditional laboratory learning as following a pre-defined script of actions, a process which by its nature leaves little space for questioning and evaluation. We have overcome this with foundation level students through a mixture of teaching approaches, including innovative, discipline-specific, open ended projects which students perform during their foundation year which address this aspect.

Stage 3: Constructing Explanations and Solutions

In this stage, based on both underlying theory and available data, students develop their own models and theories both to explain observed behaviour and to make predictions. This work leads students to develop hypotheses for testing in the laboratory, often leading them back to Stage 1 again, as this model is often adopted cyclically or in a laboratory session.

Our observations in a laboratory class indicate that students often struggle to develop beyond Stage 1, remaining focussed on the technical details. Although ensuring the quality of the data collected is vital for good science, this is often at the expense of engaging with the experiment at a deeper level, such as the behaviours seen at Stage 3. To address this, we have developed e-learning solutions that students can undertake as pre-laboratory tasks to aid them in increasing their familiarity with data collection, to allow a movement from Stage 1, through Stage 2 and to Stage 3 within the laboratory classroom or field trip. These will be outlined later, but, here, we will address our second identified barrier to laboratory learning—visualisation.

BARRIER 2: VISUALISATION

In Physics and Chemistry, many new students struggle at first to apply their learned discipline knowledge to the practical environment. This application does (when attempted) deepen their learning experience, but often the ability to correctly visualise the processes at work is a barrier to this enhancement and engagement with Stage 3. In Physics, for example, electrons flowing in wires gives us electrical lighting yet we cannot see them. In Chemistry, changes at the molecular level are imperceptible yet drive the reaction. These issues are well represented in the literature; Gilbert and Treagust (2009) for instance note that visualisation is seen as a key skill in science, yet is often neglected in science education. In Chemistry, students often struggle to bring together the macroscopic, the submicroscopic and the symbolic (the Chemistry triplet). Talanquer (2011), for example, discusses how this triplet (defined by Gilbert & Treagust, 2009) has become a central theme in science education and has shaped many curriculum projects for over some 25 years. Johnstone (1982) first highlighted the significance of this triplet relationship and pointed out that expert chemists can view their work on at least three levels. He argued that such chemists interpret chemical phenomena using a blend of the three elements of the chemistry triplet while novice learners mainly operate at the macro level and struggle to interpret phenomena meaningfully at the other levels. To work fully at Stage 3 therefore, we need to help students in the development of their ability to visualise physical processes at work. We now describe the e-learning solutions we have developed.

E-LEARNING SOLUTIONS

In outlining these e-learning solutions, we should highlight that our goal is not to replace traditional laboratory learning with simulation, as we see laboratory learning as crucial for skill development. Rather by using e-learning we aim to remove these barriers to student learning.

Overcoming Barrier 1: Preparedness

Interactive Screen Experiments (ISEs) are photograph-based virtualisations of laboratory equipment; Hatherly, Jordan and Cayless define them as "a highly interactive movie of an experiment, filmed as that experiment was being performed" (2009). Over the past decade they have evolved, following the early pioneering work of Theyssen, Aufschnaiter, and Schumacher (2002), Bacon (2004) and Kirstein and Nordmeier (2007). We have used ISEs in this project in a different form from earlier work, since here the ISEs are primarily deployed as pre-laboratory tasks to aid in overcoming a lack of practical science experience. The benefit of performing a task connected with an experiment before even entering the laboratory is well known. In relation to chemistry, for example, Johnstone and Al-Shuailib (2001) state that, "Pre-laboratory preparation is not just read your manual before you come to the laboratory, [it has] many forms, but it must prepare the student to be an active participant …"

In this work, ISEs have been developed to aid the students to feel more confident in carrying out the experiments in the laboratory safely and to have a better understanding of procedures they are undertaking. ISEs are not artificial simulations but are photograph-based Flash software, which allow the user to interact with an exact duplicate of the equipment they will be using in their next laboratory session. An ISE is then deployed within the context of a summative pre-laboratory task. Suitable experiments for ISE development have been identified, namely:

1. Foundation level Physics: The flow of electricity is best understood through practical experience, and is widely recognised as a threshold concept. This project seeks to develop a set of ISEs which allow students to build circuitry and test hypotheses before arriving at the laboratory.
2. Foundation level Chemistry: ISEs for a series of organic chemistry experiments can enable students to become familiar with techniques and concepts, such as, reflux, distillation and recrystallisation, prior to entering the laboratory. The students explore the concepts in greater depth by carrying out an experiment for which there is normally neither the time nor the equipment. An example of a part of such an ISE is shown in Fig. 5.1.
3. Foundation level Earth Science: Both mature and international foundation students frequently have little or no practical field work experience. We have noted that the complexity of the field environment may overwhelm the learner as new observations follow on rapidly and there is little time to reflect on what is being acquired.

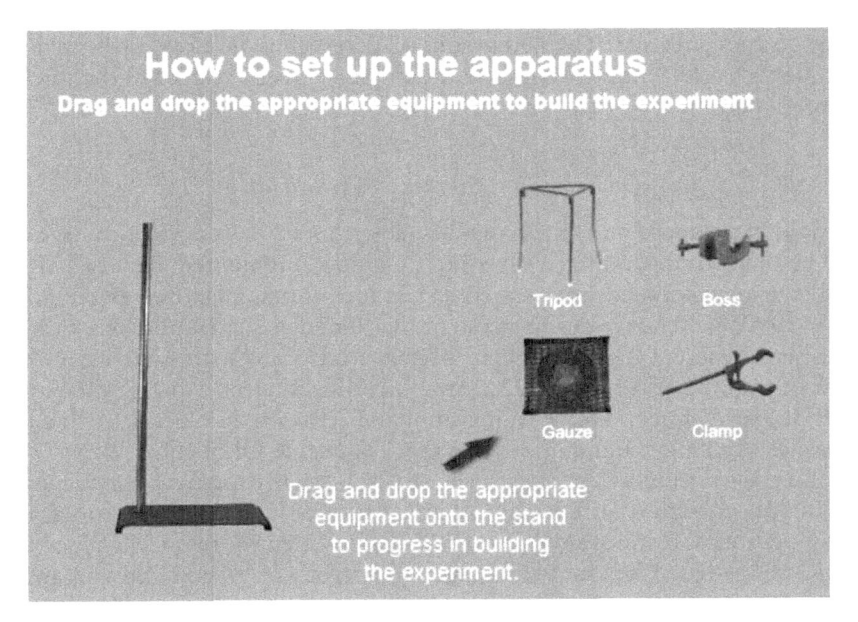

Fig. 5.1 Example of a screenshot from Chemistry ISE

Stott, Clark, Milson, McClosky, and Crompton (2009) suggested that, "Planning and practicing field skills by using the virtual resource before a visit mitigates against the effects of anxiety and improves students' confidence."

Field trips are generally of limited duration, often as short as half-a-day. The resources enable the student to develop self-paced learning so that they can familiarise themselves with the site and techniques before their visit and "hit the ground running." They can then gain more from the actual field work, because they can focus on the tasks in hand and maximise their limited time in the field. Aspects such as logistical planning, risk assessment and basic field skills can be introduced as short exercises, and this familiarisation may ease students' apprehension that arises from a fear of the unknown. The resources can also be used for reflection, revision and reinforcement after the field trip has taken place. A number of papers have reviewed the many virtual field work resources currently available (see, e.g., Litherland & Stott, 2012; Stainfield, Fisher, Ford, & Solem, 2000; Maskell et al., 2007). Such resources have a place in foundation level teaching but they are not specific to the field trips undertaken by the current students. The new resources now being developed will enable students to concentrate on information that is directly related to their field experience.

Overcoming Barrier 2: Visualisation

To aid in the adaption of the skill of visualisation, we have developed a series of interactive e-learning tools which employ Augmented Reality (AR). The term was coined by scientists at the aircraft manufacturer, Boeing, in the 1990s when developing a system that blended virtual graphics with a real environment display, to help aircraft electricians with cable assembly (as in Caudell & Mizell, 1992). At about the same time during the early 1990s, several introductory applications of AR were published, such as a surgical training programme (see Bajura, Fuchs, & Ohbuchi, 1992).

In their recent review of the uses of AR in science learning, Cheng and Tsai (2013) state that educational AR "is in its infancy" and is open to exploration and innovative application. They identify two clear types of AR: image-based and location-based. Image-based AR combines an augmented layer with natural graphics to enhance naturally occurring information, whereas location-based AR uses the location of the interacting person to enhance the information available. Here, for physics and chemistry, videos of physical or chemical systems are presented to the user with an added animated layer which may be activated to show the unobservable process at work. For physics, this could be the forces at work within a physical system, or the motion of electrons in a circuit (see Fig. 5.2).

In Fig. 5.2, by moving the slider in this simple Ohm's law experiment, students can relate voltage to the kinetic energy of electrons directly and study the relationship between resistance, current and voltage. Bernhard, Carstensen, and Holmberg (2007) have identified Ohm's laws as a complex concept (perhaps even a threshold concept) in the study of electrical circuits. Through the visualisation of electron motion, this issue, often presenting a barrier to learning, may be addressed.

For Chemistry, molecular interactions and the electron exchange underlying a particular chemical reaction are vital processes, which are often difficult to visualise. In Fig. 5.3, for example, the synthesis of Aspirin® is presented using 3D simulations produced with the modelling suite, Maya. By moving the slider at the bottom, students can zoom in from a video of a reacting vessel to a 3D visualisation of the reactants prior to interaction, and

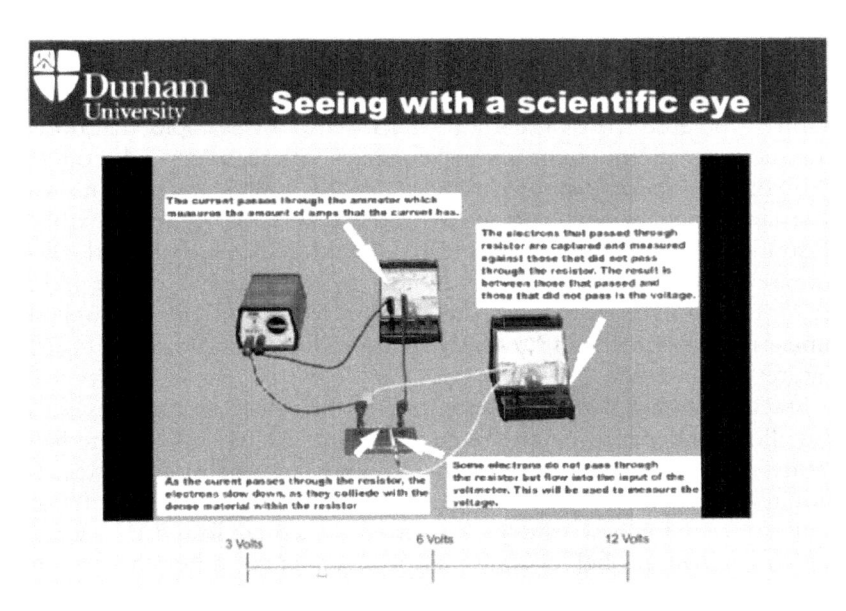

Fig. 5.2 Example of a screenshot from a Physics AR

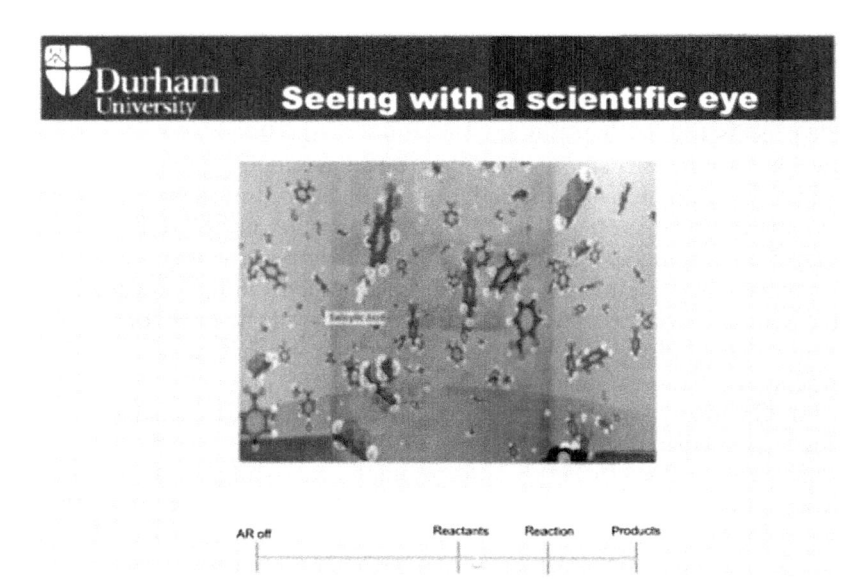

Fig. 5.3 Example of a screenshot from Chemistry AR

then on to an example of the interaction of a pair of reactants and a visualisation of the products of a reaction, which show, for example, that during a reaction, at a given instant, a vessel contains both reactants and products.

In Earth Science, one of the most difficult things for students with little field work experience is grasping the difference between textbook illustrations and the features in the field. Faults and exposures in the field are rarely "perfect" examples. An insight into what they are expected to see, draw and measure will prepare students for the difference. Similarly, familiarisation of the field sites beforehand will enable students to see the features in context.

Practice of field sketching using one of the interactive resources can also allow students to make the most of their limited time in the field. Also, familiarity with block diagrams, maps and web-based exercises should help them visualise exposures and features in 3D—often a difficult concept for new students. Stott et al. (2009) found that virtual field trip resources helped students become active rather than passive learners by using a multisensory learning ability with interactive media. The field experience can be enhanced with the use of digital microscope videos, rocks in thin section, "how to" videos and interactive tasks (Fig. 5.4).

In particular with Earth Science, being in the field is seen as a vital part of developing visualisation skills, but for some students this can be difficult. For example, foundation students taking Geography or Geology modules may have mobility and/or health problems that restrict their field work experience. While the proposed virtual field work resources will not solve this problem, they will simulate their field work learning experience to some extent. Adverse weather conditions can also limit activities in the field. Taking notes, fitting in all the tasks, engaging with the exercise and even hearing instructions or information can be difficult at times. Students working on virtual materials can work independently, in their own time and at their own pace. This also promotes foundation student's confidence and motivation.

For foundation level geology and geography, access to a number of virtual field tours enables students to gain experience of a range of field situations, some of which may be inaccessible in bad weather, subject to tides, too remote to visit, or may be in environmentally sensitive areas. While a huge range of physical geography and geology resources are available on

Fig. 5.4 Example of a screenshot from virtual field trip

the web, Litherland and Stott (2012) report that new virtual resources can provide access to local data collected by experts and amateurs with local knowledge. Links formed with professional and commercial bodies also facilitate student project opportunities.

Before looking further at the pedagogical advantages of using e-learning resources, such as those discussed above, we should mention the effort that must go into developing them. Before focussing on a qualitative analysis of their effect in the classroom, therefore, we will describe how these e-learning solutions were created.

Implementation and Analysis

One key element of this work has been the use of student developers to produce the e-learning objects. These students, themselves often former foundation level students, were employed on summer internships to develop the ISEs. This started with a series of discussions and storyboarding sessions around common issues with a given experiment and how the ISE could address these. In this sense, the ISEs were developed with the students as equal partners, as the perspective of those who have recently engaged with the subject is valuable in the development of the resources. (The resources are available for online as open educational resources (OER) at http://community.dur.ac.uk/foundation.science.)

The issues and solutions arrived at are summarised in Table 5.1 below:

Table 5.1 Summary of how each class of learning objects addresses the stages of the model (Fig. 5.1)

Approach	Issue addressed	Stage of model addressed	Subjects utilised in
Interactive screen experiments	Preparedness for laboratory study	Movement from Stage 1 to Stages 2 and 3	Physics and Chemistry
Virtual field trips	Preparedness for field trip study	Movement from Stage 1 to Stages 2 and 3	Earth Science
Augmented reality	Visualisation of non-visual physical properties of systems	Engagement with Stage 3	Physics and Chemistry

Some Evidence of the Impact of the ISEs on Learning

A series of focus groups were undertaken with foundation students. These focussed on the impact of the resources produced by this project on their learning experience. The groups comprised of a range of students, and included both local mature students and younger international students. The feedback was positive, reflected in statements such as:

> I used the screen experiment as soon as you sent it out, before the class, after the class and when I was writing the report. I hadn't done practicals in Brazil and really appreciated this.
>
> I wish we could have had more of these sent out earlier to give us something to do over the summer.

Academic staff also commented that, by using the ISEs as pre-laboratory exercises, students came to the class asking deeper questions about the subject.

The focus groups brought out two interesting observations:

> The first was that many of the international students (from countries such as China and Brazil) had little practical science experience. We found that science is taught in many countries without a strong practical element.
>
> The second observation was the students felt that, after accepting a place, they wanted to "start straight away" and they saw the ISEs as allowing them to do that.

Discussion

In her seminal work, *Rethinking University Education*, Laurillard (2002) proposed a framework for teaching based around a conversational approach between student and teacher. It is clear that one-to-one discussion between student and teacher is a potentially productive teaching approach, although it can, at times, be neither feasible nor viable. We should, perhaps, highlight the role of e-learning resources as surrogate teachers which offer, albeit in limited ways, such a "conversational framework." In *Rethinking University Education*, Laurillard examined different e-learning technologies within the context of this conversational framework, and examined how close each was to accessing its strengths. She identifies a good conversational framework as one which:

- Is an iterative dialogue between teacher and student;
- Is discursive, adaptive, interactive and reflective;
- Is at the level of descriptions of the topic;
- Is at the level of action within related tasks.

The e-learning tools developed here could be called "adaptive media," which is to say that the user (student) interacts with and affects the state of the teaching media. The tools fall in the class Laurillard identifies as "tutorial simulations" in that they possess characteristics of both tutorials and simulations. Many have argued for this blended use of e-learning technologies but Tait, has argued that the "simulations themselves are not effective learning tools, unless used to perform appropriate tasks" (1994, p. 122). For the context presented here, we suggest a slight rephrasing of Laurillard's first two conditions so that they read:

- Adaptive media must generate a constructive, iterative dialogue between teacher and student.
- Adaptive media must be discursive, adaptive, interactive, reflective and blended.

Here, the approach adopted within the framework should not be merely iterative, but constructive so that on each iteration a greater appreciation of the problem is achieved and a greater understanding of the potential solution is developed. The concepts of constructive alignment, proposed by Biggs (2003) are, therefore, clearly used. In addition, by blending many forms of discussion (in this case computer simulations and real laboratory or field work), each informs the other, and, in doing so, increases the potential for appreciation and understanding. We shall now discuss these tools in terms of the revised elements of the framework.

Adaptive Media Must Generate a Constructive Iterative Dialogue Between Teacher and Student

Media, like those described here, must aim to simulate the experiment and also to simulate the dialogue a teacher and a student would have in the laboratory. When introducing a new piece of apparatus in a laboratory, we might explain how it works and what the key buttons do. This is replicated in the ISEs when students are given explanatory pictures and photographs. The next stage in the teaching would be to set the student a task, and the ISEs do this. Where the ISE falls short, however, is in answering student questions, which a tutor would acknowledge is key to helping students learn. In this regard the student is left with a choice of (a) randomly pressing buttons until the correct answer is found (b) asking a friend or (c) waiting until the next laboratory session to ask the demonstrator. Due to the blended nature of this learning, the third choice (asking the demonstrator later in the lab) is often the practical option, which, although not ideal, allows the iterative dialogue to continue. The ISEs have been designed to be constructive in that with each task, the problem given has key components similar to the previous problem, and additional new elements.

Adaptive Media Must Be Discursive, Adaptive, Interactive, Reflective and Blended

Our use of ISEs in the Physics laboratory was originally intended as a part of the preparatory task the students do before entering the laboratory. However, we found that tutor-initiated discussion during the laboratory focussed around both the ISE and the equipment, and allowed deeper learning to take place as the students compared the real world and the simulated ISE world. Furthermore, the ISEs are by their nature adaptive and interactive, as they allow virtual interaction between student and equipment. Students then have time to reflect on their use of the ISE before being confronted with the "real" version in their next laboratory session.

Must Operate at the Level of Descriptions of the Topic

The ISE project struggles to meet this condition. Clearly the aim of ISEs, as we developed them, is to familiarise students with laboratory equipment and practice prior to using it in the lab. They are, therefore, intimately task-linked and although student discussions with each other and their tutor will connect the use of the equipment to a larger science-related aim (e.g. oscilloscopes are used to measure the speed of light in one experiment), if taken in isolation, the ISE is clearly task-heavy and topic-light. Virtual fieldtrips lie somewhere between task and topic focussed; although they include descriptions of specific tasks students must do in the field, they also include elements of theory to support this. Nevertheless, taken as a part of the whole teaching enterprise, the ISE could be said to be a part of a balanced whole.

Must Also Operate at the Levels of Action Within Related Tasks

The ISEs satisfy this condition as their aim is to introduce a piece of equipment and allow the students to engage with tasks which use the simulated equipment. This then builds directly into the laboratory session, as students can perform the same tasks and check their understanding.

In Table 5.2 below, a breakdown of each of the three e-learning tools developed against our revised conversational framework criteria is presented.

Conclusion

As has been discussed, students go through a number of significant transitions in their learning as they get used to the laboratory side of their work. For foundation students, these can be difficult due to long absences from formal education, or (in the case of international students) learning in English for the first time, or simply being relatively inexperienced in learning through practical, hands-on activities. To deepen their laboratory learning, at least two particular barriers must be overcome. First, preparation for the laboratory classroom allows students to engage more with the scientific theories being tested without focussing too heavily on the technical skills involved. Second, the ability to visualise, for example in chemistry, the molecular interactions involved whilst undertaking

Table 5.2 Summary of how each class of learning objects addresses the conversational framework of Laurillard

Framework criteria	ISE	Virtual fieldtrip	AR
Must operate a constructive iterative dialogue between teacher and student	Yes	Yes	Yes
Must be discursive, adaptive, interactive, reflective and blended	Yes	Yes	Yes
Must operate at the level of descriptions of the topic	No	Partially	Yes
Must also operate at the levels of action within related tasks	Yes	Yes	No

an experiment, deepens and enhances both engagement and learning. Through the use of e-learning resources, such as ISEs, AR and virtual field trips, we have developed open educational resources which allow students to move quickly beyond the purely technical and engage with the key science at study (and to do so in preparation for their course). This is evidenced both through responses obtained from focus groups of current students.

Acknowledgements The authors thank the Centre for Academic and Researcher Development (CARD) at Durham University for a series of funding grants through the Enhancing the Student Learning Experience Award Scheme. In addition, we have had funding through the HE STEM scheme, and workshop funding from the HEA, which have helped to develop a national network of interest in virtual experiments. We are indebted to our summer students, Andres del Castillo Dubuc, Katherine Hurst, Hannah Wynn and Takudzwa Kawanzaruwa, without whose efforts these projects would have not been possible.

REFERENCES

Bacon, R. (2004). Simulations for physics and astronomy. *LTSN Physical Science News, 5*, 10.

Bajura, M., Fuchs, H., & Ohbuchi, R. (1992). Merging virtual objects with the real world: Seeing ultrasound imagery within the patient. *ACM SIGGRAPH Computer Graphics, 26*(2), 203–210.

Bernhard, J., Carstensen, A.-K., & Holmberg, M.. (2007). *Ohm's law as a complex concept in electric circuit theory.* Proceedings of AAPT summer meeting, July 28–August 1.

Biggs, J. (2003). Aligning teaching and assessing to course objectives. *Teaching and Learning in Higher Education: New Trends and Innovations, 2*, 13–17.

Caudell, T. P., & Mizell, D. W. (1992). *Augmented reality: An application of heads-up display technology to manual manufacturing processes.* In System sciences, proceedings of the twenty-fifth Hawaii international conference (Vol. 2). Maui: IEEE.

Cheng, K., & Tsai, C.-C. (2013). Affordances of augmented reality in science learning: Suggestions for future research. *Journal of Science Education and Technology, 22*(4), 449–462.

Gilbert, J. K., & Treagust, D. F. (2009). *Multiple representations in chemical education.* London: Springer.

Hatherly, P. A., Jordan, S. E., & Cayless, A. (2009). Interactive screen experiments—Innovative virtual laboratories for distance learners. *European Journal of Physics, 30*(4), 751.

Johnstone, A. H. (1982). Macro- and micro-chemistry. *School Science Review, 64*, 377–379.

Johnstone, A., & Al-Shuailib, A. (2001). Learning in the laboratory; Some thoughts from the literature. *University Chemistry Education, 5*, 42.

Kind, P. M., & Osborne, J. (in press) Styles of scientific reasoning—A rationale for science education? *Science Education*

Kirstein, J., & Nordmeier, V. (2007). Multimedia representation of experiments in physics. *European Journal of Physics, 28*, S115.

Laurillard, D. (2002). *Rethinking university teaching: A framework for the effective use of educational technology.* London: Routledge.

Litherland, K., & Stott, T. A. (2012). Virtual field sites: Losses and gains in authenticity with semantic technologies. *Technology, Pedagogy and Education, 21*(2), 213–230.

Maskell, J., Stokes, A., Truscott, J. B., Bridge, A., Magnier, A., & Calderbank, V. (2007). Supporting fieldwork using information technology. *Planet, 18*, 18–21.

Stainfield, J., Fisher, P., Ford, B., & Solem, M. (2000). International virtual field trips: A new direction? *Journal of Geography in Higher Education, 24*(2), 255–262.

Stott, T., Clark, H., Milson, C., McClosky, J., & Crompton, K. (2009). The Ingleton Waterfalls virtual fieldtrip: Design, development and preliminary evaluation. *Teaching Earth Sciences, 34*, 13–19.

Tait, K. (1994). Discourse: The design and production of simulation-based learning environments. In T. de Jong & L. Sarti (Eds.), *Design and production of multimedia and simulation-based learning material.* Dordrecht: Kluwer.

Talanquer, V. (2011). Macro, submicro, and symbolic: The many faces of the chemistry "triplet". *International Journal of Science Education, 33*(2), 179–195.

Theyssen, H., Aufschnaiter, S. V., & Schumacher, D. (2002). *Development and evaluation in a laboratory course in physics for medical students, teaching and learning in the science laboratory.* Dordrecht: Kluwer.

CHAPTER 6

Selecting Mature Learners: A Toolkit for Admissions Tutors

Ian Moreton

WIDENING PARTICIPATION AND THE IMPORTANCE OF MATURE STUDENTS

At least in large parts of the West, there is a belief that we should be trying to build a society in which as many people as possible are free to make choices about how they live and free to achieve their potential. The fairest and most acceptable way to achieve this is through HE (Schwartz, 2004, p. 3). This is, of course, an ideological viewpoint stemming from a belief in individual freedom and may not be agreeable in all societies but here, in the UK, widening participation (WP) in HE is at the heart of government policy and embedded in universities' agreements with the Office for Fair Access (OFFA). In a recent report by Alan Milburn (2012), it is argued that every UK university needs to be actively engaged in initiatives to widen participation and make access to its institution fairer. Both engagement with the community—outreach activities—and admissions processes are seen as areas in which universities can improve their WP performance. This focus on WP is not new. Universities have always sought ways of widening their appeal; their survival and growth has depended on finding new students (more broadly, income) beyond the groups

I. Moreton (✉)
Foundation Centre, University of Durham, Pelaw House, Leazes Road, Durham DH1 1TA, UK

© The Editor(s) (if applicable) and The Author(s) 2016
C.A. Marshall et al. (eds.), *Widening Participation, Higher Education and Non-Traditional Students*,
DOI 10.1057/978-1-349-94969-4_6

already represented. The label "widening participation" that is used here, though, is more recent, having emerged as a recognised driving force for policies over the last two decades (Higher Education Funding Council for England, 1996; Schwartz Report, 2004). Its recognition as an important mechanism for social mobility is well established (Brennan & Naidoo, 2008; Panel on Fair Access to the Professions, 2009). Economic expansion in the mid-twentieth century created more opportunity, more "room at the top" and access to HE became essential for attaining the credentials needed to take advantage of the opportunities which arose. This trend has continued, and today these credentials are essential if an individual is to have a realistic chance of career progression within the "knowledge economy."

Non-traditional students, the targets of WP initiatives, are students who are in groups under-represented in HE. A number of such groups are easily identified, including:

- Members of lower socioeconomic groups (LSEs)
- Students with disabilities
- Mature students
- Members of some ethnic minority groups

Other groups may be identified from time to time, such as students from a care background, ex-services personnel and so on. Tight (2012) suggests that these groups represent the large majority of the adult population, making it perfectly clear that those groups who were traditionally represented in HE were, in fact, an elite minority.

Although these groups of non-traditional students are labelled separately, there are frequent overlaps. A mature member of an ethnic minority group with a disability, for example, can be categorised in a number of ways. Some of the overlaps that occur are of particular interest when considering the importance of one particular group. As we see in the example given, mature students may also be a part of other significant groups. A mature student who is also a member of a lower socioeconomic group (LSE) is likely to be categorised as mature, but unlikely to be included statistically in the LSE group because of the way in which institutions gather data, often relying on information about parental income and neighbourhood participation. Students who are admitted to degree programmes using WP criteria are not labelled as such, so statistics, which rely on using a range of criteria that might suggest a disadvantaged background, may not truly reflect the progress that has been made with WP initiatives (Hoare & Johnston, 2011). Opportunities for access to HE for mature students, then, have the added benefit of allowing academically able men and women from LSEs, as well as from a wide variety of backgrounds, to graduate as adults, when the disadvantages faced in adolescence may no longer present barriers (Egerton, 2000). There is also some evidence that it may be helpful to provide additional sub-categories within the mature student group. Mature students for undergraduate courses are defined as those being over 21 at the beginning of the course, but Baxter and Hatt (1999) suggest that students who are over 25 and returning to education have better outcomes than students between 21 and 25, whose education has been interrupted. They argue for the disaggregation of this group into "old and young mature students."

It is for mature students that foundation programmes are particularly useful, providing a pathway into a degree course for those who lack the required levels of skills or attainment for direct entry. In his University Challenge report, Alan Milburn (2012, p. 54) affirms that foundation year courses are "particularly helpful in equipping students from non-traditional backgrounds with the skills necessary to succeed at university," citing The Foundation Centre at Durham University as "a superb example." Figures from academic years 2010, 2011, 2012 and 2013 show that The Foundation Centre, which accounted for an average of 4.3% of the university's yearly undergraduate admissions over these cycles, provided 41.1% of the university's mature entrants.

Getting In: The Admissions Process

Admissions, the process by which students are recruited, selected and offered places at university, has been described as a "gap" between raising aspirations and the transition to HE (Graham & Shaffer, 2011). It is vitally important, particularly for WP students who may be more easily discouraged, that the applicant experience of the admissions and transition processes is positive.

In the UK, applicants for university places are required to apply through the Universities and Colleges Admissions Service (UCAS). This places them in direct competition with all other applicants for the desired course. Although universities do engage with their local communities, often as part of initiatives to widen participation, applicants can seek access to universities anywhere in the UK. Admissions decisions are generally made by academic staff in the relevant university department, based on the information contained in the UCAS application. Key to these decisions are judgements made about an applicant's merit and potential. Academic performance is heavily emphasised as a means of assessing an applicant's merit, with published entry criteria for each course. This performance is measured using previous results such as GCSE and AS exams (although a recent study by Laws (2013) has concluded that AS results add little as predictors of final degree outcomes), and predictions of results in A levels. Alongside this, a personal statement by applicants gives them an opportunity to "sell" themselves, not only explaining their passion for the subject to be studied, but also laying out all the qualities they will bring, both to the particular course and to the wider university community. The heavy reliance on academic performance to determine who should gain entry is considered to make a significant contribution to the continuing inequity in the way in which different socioeconomic groups are represented in HE, and has been called into question in a number of ways. Students from independent schools, with better staff–pupil ratios and facilities than state schools have better A-level outcomes (Schwartz Report, 2004) and are more likely to succeed in gaining entry to the university course of their choice. This effect is more pronounced in elite institutions where entry requirements are higher, further fuelling claims of social inequity. Enhanced performance at A level by private school pupils does not, however, translate into better performance at university, at the end of which state school pupils may have better degree outcomes (Smith & Naylor, 2001).

With increasing numbers of pupils leaving secondary education with better A-level grades, the need to distinguish between them, particularly for popular courses at elite institutions, has led some groups to introduce admissions tests; these are the new tools for selecting from these high-attaining groups by testing for qualities considered particularly relevant to the course of study. The Supporting Professionalism in Admissions programme (SPA), set up as recommended by the Schwartz Report (2004), defines an admissions test as a "timed, unseen, written, paper-based or online test, usually taken in the academic year prior to admission in the summer autumn term, or at interview" (SPA, 2014).

The National Admissions Test for Law (LNAT) was introduced in 2004, and is designed to test "verbal reasoning skills, the ability to understand and interpret information, inductive and deductive reasoning abilities, and the ability to analyse information and draw conclusions" (LNAT, 2014).

For medicine, the UK Clinical Aptitude Test (UKCAT), introduced in 2006, tests aptitude and attitude rather than academic ability as this has already been tested by the A-level performance. It also has specific claims about its importance to the WP agenda:

> UKCAT is committed to achieving greater fairness in selection to medicine and dentistry and to the widening participation in medical and dental training of under-represented social groups.
> (UKCAT, 2014)

It is worth questioning how a test which has been developed to differentiate between high-performing, highly qualified candidates with recent academic experience might realistically be expected to also identify merit in candidates who have been disadvantaged in some way. Evaluation of the test continues.

There are other admissions tests designed to identify students most suited to specific courses from amongst the pool of high achievers. There are mathematics tests, history tests, English tests—the list is long and, as may be expected, the elite Oxford and Cambridge universities use more of them. SPA has worked with UCAS to provide data about the tests (SPA, 2014).

So much for the high achievers, but the concern that deserving and capable WP students may not be included in this group is very real. Students who do not have the excellent record of academic achievement on which admissions decisions are traditionally based may be capable of succeeding on a degree programme, but their educational disadvantage makes their access to such a programme less likely. Hoare and Johnston (2011, p. 25) have suggested ways in which educational disadvantage might arise:

- Personal circumstances: Access to the formal support mechanisms normally available to traditional students may be lacking, particularly for mature students. There may also be disabilities that affect the ability to study and family or employment responsibilities;
- Family or household circumstances: These include lack of resources, low value placed on education and personal growth and lack of appropriate role models;

- Neighbourhood or community: Again, low value placed on education and personal growth in the student's local environment and peer group, alongside a lack of appropriate role models; and
- Schooling: Attendance at schools where precious resources may be diverted to the maintenance of discipline and there is little experience or enthusiasm for promoting university applications, together with a general disregard amongst peers for the value of academic achievement.

Once again, there may be overlaps between the categories. For example, a mature student who attended a poorly resourced school and whose family circumstances placed little value on education is disadvantaged in a number of ways. At the point when he makes a university application, in the competitive UCAS system, these disadvantages may serve to make it particularly difficult for him to show his academic potential. Aside from qualifications, his access to guidance about writing a personal statement will be limited, as will his access to suitably qualified referees. These factors need to be taken into account by admissions staff when assessing such applications, so as to minimise barriers to satisfying requirements, as laid out in the principles of the Schwartz Report (2004).

Taking such factors into account is far from straightforward and presents significant difficulties for admissions staff. Pre-application engagement with students is particularly helpful for both sides and much time may be spent meeting potential applicants to ensure they have access to all the information they need, advise on what may be the right course for them and guide them through the process. The report of the 1994 group, *Enhancing the Student Experience* (2007, p. 16) noted how influential pre-engagement initiatives could be, suggesting that the student's experience of university goes far beyond the time actually spent there; early engagement is an important aspect of preparation for university life.

Even so, experienced admissions tutors who are skilled at identifying merit and potential outside the confines of outstanding school grades and between the lines of personal statements, when asked how they do it, have difficulty articulating the processes they use. This is problematic, first because it is difficult to pass on these skills to new staff, and second because if these processes cannot be articulated, they cannot be communicated to aspiring applicants. Transparency in admissions is another of the guiding principles that formed the core of the Schwartz report; so it is important that processes used in selecting students can be published, and in a way that can be understood by applicants. It has been suggested that achieving this goal, although given much attention by institutions, policy-making bodies and regulators, still has some way to go, and the focus needs to be on the applicant experience.

Fair Access

If we are to succeed in the WP aims of fair and wider access to HE and continue to improve the diverse nature of our student body, ways of removing barriers to access for educationally disadvantaged groups need ongoing development, informed by evidence and research. Contextual data helps institutions to identify which students may be disadvantaged in some way, and some of this data is collected and disseminated by UCAS, but it is not helpful in identifying merit and potential. If we are to identify students with merit and the potential to do well at university, but without conventional academic credentials, we need to target the qualities that contribute to student success. Personal qualities that may lead to successful outcomes are to be investigated. Before we look at these qualities, it may be helpful to give an idea of what we mean by "success."

Success in Higher Education for the Non-Traditional Student

In the context of undergraduate entry to HE, it is reasonable that success should be measured by degree outcome. Measurements such as completion of the degree programme and degree classification are appropriate. For this study, which is investigating possible predictors of outcomes for non-traditional students entering HE through a foundation programme, a measure of students' success could arguably also be their outcomes at the end of the first year of the degree course, since at this stage as well as at graduation, their outcomes can be compared with those of traditional students entering via the conventional route.

Personal Qualities

Of the "Big Five" personality descriptors—neuroticism, extraversion, conscientiousness, agreeableness and openness to experience (Digman, 1990)—the construct which has been most often linked to student success is conscientiousness. According to Trautwein, Lüdtke, Roberts,

Schnyder, and Niggli (2009), individuals who exhibit conscientiousness are characterised as being hardworking and industrious, systematic, dutiful and striving for achievement, so it is not surprising that it is the Big Five factor most commonly connected with success and achievement. Many studies have explored this connection. Noftle and Robins (2007) found that conscientiousness was a strong predictor of high school and college Grade Point Average (GPA). Wagerman and Funder (2007, p. 221) found conscientiousness to be "a valid and unique predictor of college performance." Cela-Ranilla, Gisbert and de Oliveira (2011) conclude that academic performance is positively influenced by conscientiousness. In a recent study of factors affecting academic success at Durham University's Foundation Centre, Marshall (2013, p. 36) found that "using previous study at A level for mature, non-traditional students is not the best indicator of potential, but that attitudinal attributes, specifically those correlated with conscientiousness are much better indicators of success." In The Netherlands, a study conducted by Van Bragt, Bakx, Bergen, and Croon (2010) confirmed a strong positive correlation between conscientiousness and academic performance, not only in terms of grades, but also in terms of continuance. Apart from gaining more academic credits, students with higher scores on conscientiousness were found to be less likely to drop out. The Netherlands study also found a negative correlation between academic success and students' scores on the learning conceptions of Ambivalence and Lack of Regulation. Ambivalence is described as having a variety of motivations to learn, but none in particular. Lack of Regulation describes a student who does not know what, when or why to do things. The significance of this finding is that we should be aware of possible characteristics or orientations which have negative correlations with successful outcomes, as these indicators may be as important as those which have positive correlations.

Hardiness, with its component constructs of control, commitment and challenge, has also been linked to students' success (Kobasa, 1979). Control is demonstrated by those who overcome difficulties so as to continue to exercise control over what is happening. Commitment is demonstrated by those who feel closely involved with (and committed to) their activities, so that stressful events are mitigated by a sense of purpose. Challenge is demonstrated by those who embrace, and are stimulated by, change (Maddi, 2006). A study conducted by Sheard and Golby (2007) among undergraduate students at a North-East UK university, found that the hardiness construct of commitment was significantly correlated with academic success. Overall hardiness was also found to have a moderating effect on performance but, surprisingly, challenge showed a negative correlation.

Motivation to learn is central to students' success. The motivated student's beliefs lead to constructive behaviour that focuses on what is needed to produce successful outcomes. According to Dörnyei (2001, p. 18), motivation is highest when people are competent, have sufficient autonomy, set worthwhile goals, get feedback and are affirmed by others. Vermunt (1992) described five different motivational orientations:

1. Certificate oriented: The qualification is the primary focus.
2. Vocationally oriented: The focus is on a particular career pathway and becoming a part of a community of practice.
3. Self-test oriented: The driving force is self-proof and satisfaction in extending personal capabilities.
4. Personally interested: Passion for the subject itself.
5. Ambivalent oriented: Motivation to learn exists but is not clearly defined.

Not surprisingly the last category here, ambivalence, has been shown to have a negative correlation to success as mentioned above (Van Bragt et al., 2010).

The psychological study of motivation is complex and dynamic, historically changing from a drive perspective which was biologically based, through behavioural models to a cognitive perspective. Central themes in more recent work are the role of affect and less conscious processes (Eccles, Wigfield, & Schiefele, 1998, cited in Dörnyei, 2001, p. 19). These themes are outside the scope of this study, which aims to explore relationships between personal attributes and success in HE, rather than exploring the nature and construction of the attributes themselves, but the importance of motivation as a factor influencing success cannot be overstated. A student's motivation to study will have a direct bearing on why they want to study, how long they will sustain the study and how hard they will work towards their goals.

Self-efficacy, an important mediator of motivation, has been offered as a significant factor bearing on student performance, and it should be considered along with the other factors. Described as "the belief in one's capabilities to organize and execute courses of action required to produce given attainments" (Bandura, 1997, p. 3), self-efficacy asks the question, "can I do this?". When the question is applied by a student to either distal or proximal goals, it is an essential component of motivation, and a student who answers in the negative may set lower goals. Self-efficacy is, however, subject to change through experience—particularly repetitive experience (Bandura, 1977)—so that students who are educationally disadvantaged may have lower levels of self-efficacy as a direct result of this disadvantage. Rather than using this attribute, which is linked to success (Zimmerman, 1995), as a factor to be considered when selecting students, it may be more appropriate to provide remediation within the learning and teaching process that will help to reinforce positive self-efficacy.

Self-efficacy is also a contributor to resilience, another important factor in student success. Resilience is not easy to define, but often easily recognised. Films like The Pursuit of Happyness [sic], based on the life of Chris Gardner who, while caring for his five-year-old son, battled with homelessness and destitution as he worked to make a better life for them, lives of public figures like Nelson Mandela who inspired a generation worldwide and fairy tales like *Cinderella* all present us with characters who display resilience. They succeed "against the odds," so that we admire them and are drawn to them. As well as showing self-efficacy, resilient individuals tend to be optimistic and goal-oriented, have coping skills and take personal responsibility for actions and outcomes. According to Wang, Haertel, Walberg, and Mid-Atlantic Lab. for Student Success and National Research Center on Education in the Inner Cities (1998, p. 3), resilient individuals exhibit a high level of engagement and a sense of "personal agency." Their study goes on to underline the link between these qualities and educational attainment.

Phenomenography

As we have seen, a review of the literature has provided a variety of evidence about what contributes to a student's success in HE, but it would be a mistake to ignore another rich source of valuable information. Foundation centre staff have a wealth of experience in teaching, guiding and mentoring non-traditional students, and their conceptions, based on this wealth of experience, of what characteristics contribute to successful outcomes for students, can be a valuable addition to this study. Students themselves may also have a valid contribution to make based on their own reflections. It may also be of interest to explore conceptions of what may be needed for success among pre-application students, that is, those who are beginning to engage with a foundation centre for information, advice and guidance. These three disparate groups may be expected to have quite different conceptions, with experienced foundation centre staff having a more considered and authoritative voice. Exploring all three voices was considered important, to add depth and balance to the study.

Method

Gathering data of this type, in which participants' conceptions are explored, has been successfully accomplished using Marton's (1981) phenomenographic method (e.g. Newton & Newton, 2009), and it is this method that was used here. Participants were interviewed and their responses recorded. To ensure minimum influence on the responses of the participants, there was no preparatory questionnaire and interviewees were asked to respond to the question: What qualities are important for a non-traditional student to be successful in HE? Some adjustment to the question was made when interviewing students, so as to ensure there was no confusion about what was meant by "non-traditional students." In these cases, the question was couched in terms that enabled the interviewee to identify himself or herself in relation to the question. Interviewing techniques were used to elicit maximum response, clarifying and extending, without influencing the content of that response. Most interviews lasted 10–15 minutes. Responses were then transcribed from notes and audio recordings into a series of statements. Those statements, colour coded to indicate their origin (colleague/current student/potential student) and printed separately, became the data pool. Included in this pool were, for example, "An attitude that does not expect to be spoon-fed with answers," "My motivation was the children—I want to inspire them," "Almost anybody has the ability, if the circumstances are right, to get a degree."

Using an iterative process as described by Newton and Newton (2009), the pool was sorted, then resorted into groups containing statements with something in common. The resorting process led to the evolution of groups that were "self-consistent and mutually exclusive." The groups were labelled and their characteristics listed. These groups, then, formed the categories of description described by Marton (1981).

Results

The categories of description that emerged from the sorting of the data pool were in two groups:

1. *Driving Force*:

- Interest in what they want to study
- Interest in learning
- Desire to improve themselves
- A need for change

Included in this category are both intrinsic and extrinsic motivation.

2. *Certain Assets*:

- Genetic endowment such as intelligence
- Habits of mind such as conscientiousness, persistence and determination
- Self-beliefs such as self-efficacy
- Acquired "skills" such as thinking and learning skills, emotion coping skills, knowledge and knowhow

There is insufficient space here to list the details of responses in each category; some example responses are included above. Surprisingly, there were many similarities between the responses of the three disparate groups of interviewees, although the degree of sophistication in describing concepts was, understandably, varied.

Towards a Toolkit

This chapter has no conclusion, because the work is ongoing and real conclusions are yet to be reached. Having reviewed some of the literature and collected concepts of what it takes to be a successful student from colleagues, current students and potential students, the work of producing a toolkit for use by admissions selectors has begun. During induction, students enrolling on courses at the Foundation Centre were invited to complete a questionnaire designed to gauge conscientiousness, self-efficacy and resilience, motivation and grit (hardiness). Results from this survey, combined with the outcomes of the phenomenographical study and evidence from the literature, will be compared with students' results at various stages, both during their year at the Foundation Centre and beyond. It is hoped that relationships that emerge between those personal qualities suggested by responses to this and any future survey, and a student's success in HE, will help to inform future practice. It should be emphasised, however, that all efforts will be made to avoid creating new and artificial barriers to entry for the very non-traditional students we are seeking to support. The toolkit, consisting of "measures" of the characteristics found to be potentially useful, is intended not as a means of selection, but as a means by which selectors can make informed decisions at all stages of the admissions process. Early indications are that selection will be best accomplished by selectors who are experts in the field. The successful Physics student, for example, may have different personal qualities to the successful Sociology student. It is anticipated that "measures" which form the toolkit will inform the intuition of these expert selectors as they make their decisions.

REFERENCES

1994 Group of Universities. (2007). *Enhancing the student experience: Policy report.* Available at http://www.1994group.ac.uk/studentexperience.php

Bandura, A. (1977). Self-efficacy: Toward a unifying theory of behavioural change. *Psychological Review, 84,* 191–215.

Bandura, A. (1997). *Self-efficacy: The exercise of control.* New York: W.H.Freeman and Company.

Baxter, A., & Hatt, S. (1999). Old and young mature students: Painting a fuller picture. *Journal of Access and Credit Studies, 1*(2), 137–148.

Brennan, J., & Naidoo, R. (2008). Higher education and the achievement (and/or prevention) of equity and social justice. *Higher Education, 56,* 287–302.

Cela-Ranilla, J. M., Gisbert, M., & de Oliveira, J. M. (2011). Exploring the relationship among learning patterns, personality traits, and academic performance in freshmen. *Educational Research and Evaluation, 17*(3), 175–192.

Digman, J. M. (1990). Personality structure: Emergence of the 5-factor model. *Annual Review of Psychology, 41,* 417–440.

Dörnyei, Z. (2001). *Teaching and researching motivation.* Harlow: Longman.

Eccles, J., Wigfield, A., & Schiefele, A. (1998). Motivation to succeed. In W. Damon & N. Eisenberg (Eds.), *Handbook of child psychology, 5th edition, vol.*

3: *Social, emotional and personality development* (pp. 1017–1095). New York: Wiley.

Egerton, M. (2000). Monitoring student flows and characteristics: Secondary analyses using the labour force survey and the general household survey. *Journal of the Royal Statistical Society Series A – Statistics in Society, 163*, 63–80.

Graham, J., & Shaffer, D. (2011). Working together on widening access, admissions and transition into higher education. In M. Tight (Ed.), *International perspectives on higher education research, vol. 6: Institutional transformation to engage a diverse student body* (pp. 155–168). Available from: doi:10.1108/S1479-3628(2011)0000006016

Higher Education Funding Council for England. (1996). *Widening access to higher education: A report by HEFCEs advisory group on access and participation.* Available at: http://webarchive.nationalarchives.gov.uk/20100202100434/http://www.hefce.ac.uk/pubs/hefce/1996/m9_96.htm

Hoare, A., & Johnston, R. (2011). Widening participation through admissions policy: A British case study of school and university performance. *Studies in Higher Education, 36*(1), 21–41.

Kobasa, S. C. (1979). Stressful life events, personality, and health: An inquiry into hardiness. *Journal of Personality and Social Psychology, 37*(1), 1–11.

Laws, D. (2013). *A comparison of GCSE and AS level results as a predictor of getting a 2:1 or above at University.* Available at: https://www.gov.uk/government/uploads/system/uploads/attachment_data/file/200903/GCSE_and_AS_level_Analysis_3_1.pdf. Accessed 15 August 2014.

LNAT. (2014). Available at: http://www.lnat.ac.uk. Accessed 29 August 2014.

Maddi, S. (2006). Hardiness: The courage to grow from stresses. *Journal of Positive Psychology, 1*, 160–168.

Marshall, C. (2013). Good foundations: Prediction of degree success in non-traditional students. *Widening Participation and Lifelong Learning, 15*(2), 22–42.

Marton, F. (1981). Phenomenography: Describing conceptions of the world around us. *Instructional Science, 10*, 177–200.

Milburn, A. (2012). *University challenge: How higher education can advance social mobility.* London: Cabinet Office.

Newton, D. P., & Newton, L. D. (2009). Some student teachers' conceptions of creativity in school science. *Research in Science Technological Education, 27*(1), 45–60.

Noftle, E., & Robins, R. (2007). Personality predictors of academic outcomes: Big five correlates of GPA and SAT scores. *Journal of Personality and Social Psychology, 93*(1), 116–130.

Panel on Fair Access to the Professions. (2009). *Unleashing aspiration.* London: Cabinet Office.

Schwartz Report. (2004). Fair admissions to higher education: Recommendations for good practice. Available at http://www.admissions-review.org.uk/consultation.html

Sheard, M., & Golby, J. (2007). Hardiness and undergraduate academic study: The moderating role of commitment. *Personality and Individual Differences, 43*, 579–588.

Smith, J., & Naylor, R. (2001). Determinants of degree performance in UK universities: A statistical analysis of the 1993 student cohort. *Oxford Bulletin of Economics and Statistics, 63*, 29–60.

SPA. (2014). Supporting professionals in admissions, Available at: http://www.spa.ac.uk/information/admissionstests/. Accessed 14 August 2014.

Tight, M. (2012). *Researching higher education*. Maidenhead: Open University Press.

Trautwein, U., Lüdtke, O., Roberts, B., Schnyder, I., & Niggli, A. (2009). Different forces, same consequence: Conscientiousness and competence beliefs are independent predictors of academic effort and achievement. *Journal of Personality and Social Psychology, 97*(6), 1115–1128.

UKCAT. (2014). *What is the UKCAT?* Available at: http://www.ukcat.ac.uk/about-the-test. Accessed 21 August 2014.

Van Bragt, C., Bakx, A., Bergen, T., & Croon, M. (2010). Looking for students' personal characteristics predicting study outcome. *Higher Education, 61*, 59–75.

Vermunt, J. (1992). *Learning styles and guidance of learning processes in higher education*. Amsterdam: Lisse Swets and Zeitlinger.

Wagerman, S., & Funder, D. (2007). Acquaintance reports of personality and academic achievement: A case for conscientiousness. *Journal of Research in Personality, 41*, 221–229.

Wang, M., Haertel, G., Walberg, H., & Mid-Atlantic Lab. for Student Success and National Research Center on Education in the Inner Cities. (1998). *Educational resilience*. Publication series No. 11, ERIC, EBSCOhost, viewed 21 August 2014.

Zimmerman, B. J. (1995). Self-efficacy and educational development. In A. Bandura (Ed.), *Self-efficacy in changing societies* (pp. 202–231). Cambridge: Cambridge University Press.

CHAPTER 7

Challenges and Opportunities in Using Facebook to Build a Community for Students at a UK University

Nick Pearce and Sarah Learmonth

SOCIAL MEDIA AND UNIVERSITY RECRUITMENT

Facebook offers a low-cost, scalable platform for interacting with a huge audience. For universities, this audience can encompass potential, current and past students. Facebook has emerged as a prominent social media interface that HEIs are utilising to interact and recruit potential students; it provides a space for informal and formal communication among students, and between students and universities. This chapter will explore current research into the influence of social media on student choice of university and provide a case study of a formal presence for Durham University Foundation Centre, which was launched in 2010. This experience will

---

N. Pearce (✉)
Foundation Centre, University of Durham, Pelaw House, Leazes Road, Durham DH1 1TA, UK

S. Learmonth
Institute of Criminology, University of Cambridge, Sidgwick Avenue, Cambridge CB3 9DA, UK

© The Editor(s) (if applicable) and The Author(s) 2016
C.A. Marshall et al. (eds.), *Widening Participation, Higher Education and Non-Traditional Students*,
DOI 10.1057/978-1-349-94969-4_7

form the basis of a more general discussion of the challenges and opportunities which Facebook presents.

Facebook is part of a growing phenomenon of social media technology; this can be referred to as "web-based and mobile applications that allow individuals and organizations to create, engage, and share new user-generated or existing content, in digital environments through multi-way communication" (Davis III, Deil-Amen, Rios-Aguilar, & Gonzalez Canche, 2012, p. 1). Facebook is one of the most popular social media technologies (Boyd & Ellison, 2008), with two-thirds of online adults using Facebook (Duggan & Brenner, 2013). Users can access Facebook through their computers and mobile devices, where they can control a user-generated profile, interact with contacts and engage with interests of their choosing; users can also join communities on pages or groups and use features such as chat or gaming. Facebook has created an ever-widening digital environment, with no immediate competitors that pose a threat to its dominant position as one of the most used online services globally. It has nearly 1 billion monthly users as of June 2012, with more than 500 million active daily (Allen, 2012).

It is not surprising that with 1 billion users globally, it has permeated into all other aspects of society, including education. A review of 24 leading British research-intensive universities' presence on Facebook found that as of July 2014 their Facebook pages had between 20,000 and 1.5 million fans, with a total of 3.6 million (Kelly, 2014). It is now "ever present in HE, in the lecture theatre, the classroom, the library, the halls of residence and the student union" (Stirling, 2014, p. 30). Presence can be seen in a multitude of ways: a tool for informal and formal learning and teaching, a platform to allow students to engage with the broader university and colleges, and courses are now being widely advertised on Facebook (Kent & Leaver, 2014).

Barnes and Mattson (2009) completed studies to document the usage of social media by US colleges and universities when recruiting prospective students; in 2008, 85% of college admission offices were using at least one form of social media. There is recognition that social media technologies have great potential to complement existing strategies of student recruitment (Wandel, 2008). This is because Facebook, and other similar social media platforms, can create the "network effect"; information can spread and flow online in a manner different to traditional recruiting techniques, allowing potential students to make informed decisions (Gosh, Chawla, & Mallott, 2012).

Hayes, Ruschman, and Walker (2009) concluded from a case study that there was a significant relationship between those who logged onto a university social networking system and the likelihood of them applying to the university. Constantinides and Zinck Stagno (2012) suggest this is a reasonable assumption; prospective students who engage with social media platforms as part of a university recruitment strategy could contribute to increased applications and help prospective students make better-informed decisions regarding their study choice and university selection. Yet it is acknowledged that little is known about the impact of social media on the decision-making process of future students regarding their choice for study and university. Despite this lack of knowledge on the relationship between social media platforms and prospective students, socially oriented digital media has become a powerful tool due to the ability to connect students and cultivate a sense of community among them (McLoughlin & Lee, 2014). Facebook can create an engaging, inexpensive way to interact with prospective and current students alongside alumni.

The Foundation Centre provides a "year 0" preparation for international and domestic mature students who go on to take the full range of degree programmes at Durham University. They therefore represent a particularly diverse group. The Centre has been operating since 1997 and in the year 2013–14 had approximately 200 students, from 33 countries. This provides a manageable community of present and past students which could be targeted through a Facebook page, as well as providing a potential tool for presenting the Centre to prospective students (for more of the rationale for establishing the page, see Pearce, 2010).

This chapter will present a case study of the creation of a Facebook page for the Foundation Centre at Durham University over four years to inform a discussion of some of the issues which arise from creating an official presence on the site and enable a discussion of particular student groups and how they are interacting with the page.

Investigating Facebook Use

From its outset Facebook has been at the centre of debates about privacy (e.g. Albrechtslund, 2008; Grimmelmann, 2009). These debates focus around the extent to which individuals participate in an exchange whereby they agree to give up some of their privacy in order to benefit from the information shared by others in their network. For Albrechtslund, this is a new form of participatory surveillance which has positive benefits as "a way to voluntarily engage with other people and construct identities" (2008, p. 7). Whether or not this is the case for all individuals on Facebook is open to debate, but the key concern for this chapter is the recognition that individuals knowingly share some of their personal information in order to participate in the social network. From a methodological point of view, the question becomes, to what extent is this information, or a subset of it, a legitimate source of data?

A substantial project (see Parry, 2011; Zimmer, 2010) which produced a longitudinal dataset of Facebook profile and network information of an entire university course, over a four-year period, ignited considerable debate over the ethics of research into this area. This project used student researchers who made their networks available to researchers, who could then trace the interconnections of a class. This issue initiated a debate about the privacy of the members of those networks, who had not explicitly consented to take part in the study, and whose anonymity could not be ensured.

The analysis carried out in this case study is with the information shared with the page, rather than another individual, and all of the information taken from Facebook is publicly viewable, and therefore does not violate the individual's privacy as such, although no students or staff are mentioned by name in this paper (Parry, 2011).

Using social media in education brings with it the relative ease with which large amounts of data can be gathered, and this has spawned a new sub-discipline of webometrics (Thelwall, 2008). Facebook provides page administrators access to a reasonable amount of anonymised demographic data about the users and quantitative historic information about the interactions such as the number of likes, wall postings or photo views. These data can be exported as a spreadsheet and this has been used as the basis for some of the analyses in the next section. This information was explored further in a number of ways to provide more relevant data for this case study.

One key question that this chapter seeks to address is, to what extent the Foundation Centre's Facebook page has been successful in engaging with future, current and past students? Originally, the aim had been to classify which community our fans belonged to by extracting the list of people who liked the page and cross-referencing against an internal student database in order to identify current and past students. Staff members and other Facebook pages that had liked our page were identified (such as the University's International Office). The assumption was made that the remaining fans would be prospective students. This is likely to be an overestimate and some of these may have liked the page for other reasons, but it seems unlikely that there would be many who would have liked the page for alternative reasons.

A difficulty arose with this approach due to recent changes in privacy settings on Facebook which allow users to remain absent from the fan list of a page, making it challenging to ascertain a true reflection of which community they belong to. Whilst users can remain hidden from the list, their username is available should they opt to interact with the page. Therefore, an alternative approach was taken. Data were extracted from the last 12 months of interactions (messages, likes, comments and shares) which was then cross-referenced across the internal student database in order to identify current and past students. Remaining fans were assumed to be prospective, once staff members and other pages were identified.

Case Study: Foundation Centre on Facebook

The initial proposal for establishing the page suggested that it could create an online community with three key audiences identified: prospective students, current students and alumni. This focus on community and range of potential users, allied with the relative ease in setting up and monitoring the page, led to a *laissez faire* attitude when the page was set up in October 2010. From August 2013, a student was employed as a social media assistant on a part-time basis to manage the Foundation Centre's social media presence.

Prior to the establishment of the Facebook page there had been an effort to establish an online community for current students, through setting up a space in the virtual learning environment (VLE), based on Blackboard, called "Foundation Family" to share photos from social events and comments. This had struggled to gain momentum and had been abandoned by the time the Facebook page had been set up. There are a number of issues with attempting to create a community within a VLE which this highlights. First, the VLE is generally accessed by students only for specific academic-related uses such as downloading PowerPoint slides and is not generally visited on a regular basis. This also means that the environment is closely associated with academic work, which makes it a difficult location to foster a more informal community. In addition to this, only current students of the university have accounts for the VLE,

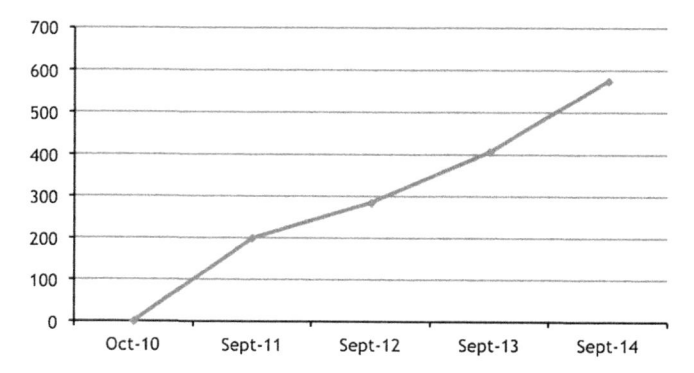

Fig. 7.1 Total likes on Facebook during project lifetime

making it impossible to interact with prospective students and difficult to interact with past students once they have graduated.

Another rationale for establishing the Facebook page was that there was the possibility of a third party creating their own page or group for the Centre over which the staff would have no control. Whilst this informality about the Facebook space is popular with students, it can complicate the University's use of it (Madge, Meek, Wellens, & Hooley, 2009). Creating an official page would enable an element of control over its content and direction.

Figure 7.1 shows the cumulative total likes which the page has recorded to date. As you can see there was quite a rapid start. The page was initially promoted in an email to all students and staff, and since then has been promoted through a link in the web page (our most common referrer) as well as being found through Google (our second most common referrer). Given the social nature of Facebook it would be expected that this would be a source of new likes as photos have been uploaded and tagged or as items have appeared in the news feeds of non-fans. Growth slowed between September 2011 and September 2012; a possible explanation could be the lack of relevant content due to the *laissez-faire* approach prior to the appointment of a social media assistant. There has since been a steady growth of new likes, with a 40.9% increase in the period between September 2013 and September 2014.

Having outlined some general information about the level of use, the next question is, who is using the site? (Fig. 7.2) One consistent feature

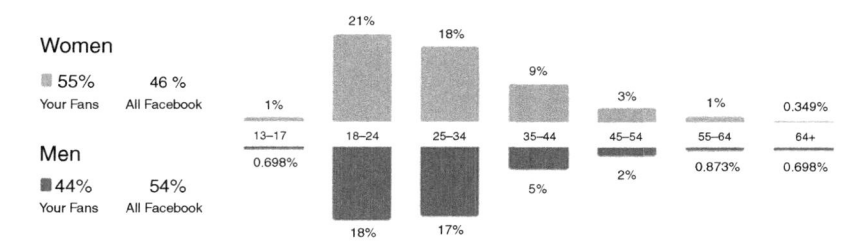

Fig. 7.2 Demographic data

from the outset of the Facebook page has been a majority (55%) of female users. This has been fairly consistent over the lifetime of the page; the figure was 61% in 2012 and 58% in 2013. The number of male users has gradually increased, resulting in a more even distribution of users. An analysis of the student database suggests that 53% of students since 1997 have been female, but if we take the last four years, only 42% have been female, so female participation with the Facebook page is more than would be expected given the known properties of the current and past student cohorts.

The age demographic is also more evenly spread than you might expect for a student group, but this would reflect not only the more diverse student body at the Foundation Centre, but also the inclusion of alumni from previous cohorts.

It would have been interesting to explore the nationality of the page fans but whilst Facebook provides information on nationality; this is based on the Facebook settings which the individual sets and are clearly vulnerable to international students setting up their accounts upon arrival in the UK and appearing as UK-based. This effect would be particularly pronounced for students from countries where Facebook and other social media sites are banned or restricted (such as China at the present time), where creating an account prior to arrival is very difficult if not impossible.

In order to explore how categories of students, whether potential, past or current students, were interacting with the page, data was extracted from a 12-month period and examined further. This sample ranged from 25 September 2013 to 25 September 2014, to incorporate both the academic year and activity over vacations. Interactions were considered to be messages received to the inbox, likes on any content including photos, comments and shares. This excluded multiple exchanges of dialogue after an initial message was received; therefore, the interaction was counted as 1, regardless of further messages received from the same individual in response to staff.

Interactions were required to be extracted manually. Facebook does provide the option to download data such as key page metrics. However, this information is only accessible for the last 180 days, rendering it unsuitable for any longer term analysis. Each individual interaction was identified; this was achieved by using the timeline feature to locate all content that had been posted by either the page directly or by fans. The type of interaction was not recorded; instead the name of the fan was noted within a Microsoft Excel file. This did result in the name of some fans being recorded more than once, or several times depending on how often they interacted with the page. This could potentially result in some categories being skewed due to fans that are exceptionally active on a Facebook page. However, this did not appear to be the case when reviewing the results.

Once this information was collated, the names were then cross-referenced with the internal student database in order to identify current and past students, and what year they joined the Foundation Centre. Remaining fans were assumed to be prospective, once staff members and other Facebook pages were identified. However, it is recognised that some interactions may have come from family members of fans (e.g. a family member may "like" a photograph of a fan from a Foundation Centre event); therefore, the volume of prospective students is likely to be overestimated. Once all the fans were assigned a category, it was felt an extra category would be beneficial to data analysis as this allowed for a detailed understanding of who is interacting with the page; therefore, an additional category was created of "2014—pre-arrival." All prospective students were cross-referenced against an internal student database to confirm whether they had accepted a placement at the Foundation Centre and were due to enrol in October 2014 (Fig. 7.3).

A significant number of those interacting with the page were current students. These are students who entered the Foundation Centre in 2013. An explanation of this could be related to promotion of the Facebook page to students when they arrive, and before. Additionally, the Foundation Centre staff have utilised social media by combining induction events with the Facebook page. For example, it was encouraged that students upload

Year of Entry

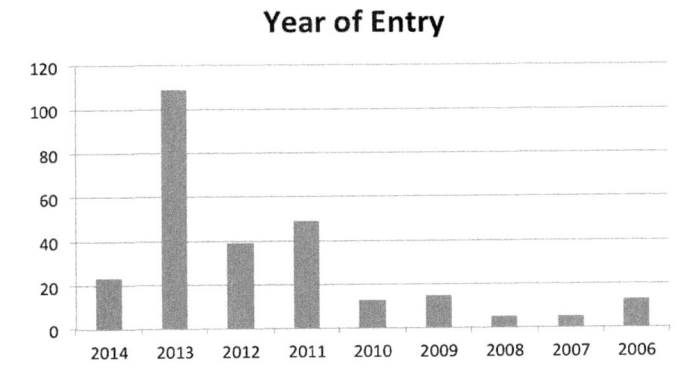

Year	Count
2014	~22
2013	~110
2012	~40
2011	~50
2010	~14
2009	~16
2008	~7
2007	~7
2006	~15

Fig. 7.3 Year of entry

photographs of Durham to enter into a competition to win university merchandise. Other events during the academic year were photographed and uploaded on the page with students being encouraged to share and tag their classmates.

Twenty-three students were identified as pre-arrival for 2014 entry. This is likely to increase when the academic year begins, for the reasons described above. The reasons for a pre-arrival student interacting with the page include ascertaining further information such as transport, living arrangements or financial enquiries. When exploring the level of interactions from the alumni category, there is a noticeable increase from 2011, with 49 student interactions recorded and 39 students from the 2012 cohort. It is important to note that the page was set up in October 2010; therefore it is encouraging that alumni prior to this date have not only joined the page but have also interacted with the page regularly (Fig. 7.4).

When analysing the overall breakdown of interactions by all categories over a 12-month period, alumni and prospective students engaged with the page more than current students. Whilst current students did interact with the page significantly as identified in Fig. 7.3, this was still less than all alumni (2006–2012) and prospective students (excluding the 2014 pre-arrival category). This could suggest that the initial aim to set up a Facebook page to create an online community has been achieved due to the similar level of interactions from each category.

■ Alumni ■ Prospective ■ Staff ■ 2014 pre arrival ■ Current

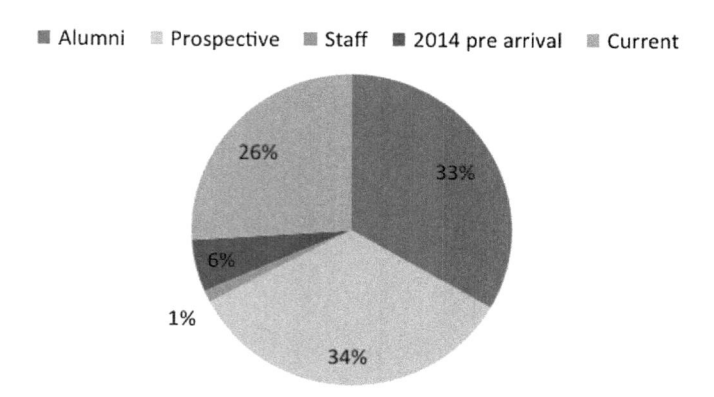

- 33%
- 26%
- 6%
- 1%
- 34%

Fig. 7.4 Categories of fans

REFLECTIONS: CHALLENGES AND OPPORTUNITIES

From the start, an early concern among staff was about privacy and the blurring of professional boundaries with students. These are two slightly different issues. The first relates to unease that staff had about the potential for sharing their private profiles with students, and also about appearing to invade the private space of students; the second is the related but separate issue of how Facebook has established itself as a private, informal space and a worry that students would either resist the Foundation Centre encroaching on this, or that the page might be seen to erode the professional standing of staff.

By liking the Facebook page, the individual is not sharing their private information with the page administrators or other fans apart from their username and profile picture. Similarly, when those staff members who have been designated as administrators interact with the page they do so as the page itself, rather than as their individual profiles, and therefore they do not share their personal information (including their username or profile picture) with the rest of the page community. Whilst the administrator can change whether they are interacting with the page in a personal capacity or not, many forget to do this or are unaware and this can lead to some personal comments posted as if through the page profile.

As for the Facebook page encroaching on the individual's privacy, the experience to date appears to be the opposite. Clearly users who felt that liking the Facebook page would share their personal information with it, and who had an issue with this, would not like the page in the first place, and so the success of the page in gaining fans suggests that this has not been the case. In fact, an issue that has arisen recently has been prospective students posting enquiries onto the wall about their particular applications which has started conversations which Centre staff have felt would be better continued in private. It seems that for some prospective students at least they are too keen to share details of their applications, and that rather than worry about the page encroaching on their privacy, the page is worried about their lack of privacy. So far, the Centre has responded to this on an *ad hoc* basis, but it is clear that there is a need for a clear privacy policy which establishes which conversations are best had in private and which are best had in public and takes into account any legal issues (Grimmelmann, 2009; JISC, 2011).

It is important to recognise that Facebook is a business and this consequently has practical implications. Facebook generates income through placing targeted adverts, and as the Foundation Centre page is recognised as an educational page, frequented by students, the adverts can be from competing providers. A further practical consideration is that the business model for Facebook can change at any time and that if the Foundation Centre is committed to maintaining a presence this may incur additional costs in the future (e.g. if pages became a "freemium" feature, subject to charges for additional functionality).

Another initial challenge to creating and maintaining an effective presence on Facebook was the time commitment required to post and respond to content. Originally this had been managed through staff time, but this was not ideal as the page continued to expand, and as the Centre looked to expand its presence onto other media (e.g. Twitter) this was not sustainable. A decision was made to employ a student as a social media intern on a part-time contract to assist with this. This is a strategy that is being used across the UK and the USA and provides for an excellent job opportunity for the student as well as providing an enthusiastic source of content for the page.

A final challenge is to realise that despite the apparent dominance of Facebook its coverage is not total. An increasing number of users have rejected or are rejecting the space and other social spaces exist where students create their own communities (Rainie, Smith, & Duggan, 2013). In the Foundation Centre context one such space has been created by our students on the website The Student Room (http://www.thestudentroom.co.uk/showthread.php?t=2328693). Similarly, access to Facebook is restricted in some countries, which is especially important for a centre which is attempting to recruit international students from places like China and Vietnam.

A Multi-Channel Future

This case study has been able to provide a snapshot of the way that prospective and current students and alumni connect with the page for a one-year programme over a four-year period.

It is clear that Facebook is a useful medium for many students, and for our centre to promote itself, although it is important to remember those who are not on Facebook, and who do not rely exclusively on this, or any other social media, to interact with these groups. Facebook is a low-cost and attractive platform for interacting with students, but it should not be relied on as the only platform for any community-building strategy.

References

Allen, M. (2012). An education in Facebook. *Digital Culture & Education*, 4(3), 213–225.

Albrechtslund, A. (2008). Online social networking as participatory surveillance. *First Monday* 13(3).

Barnes, N. G., & Mattson, E. (2009). *Social media and college admissions: The first longitudinal study*. Center for Marketing Research. Dartmouth.

Boyd, d., & Ellison, N. B. (2008). Social network sites: Definition, history, and scholarship. *Journal of Computer-Mediated Communication*, 13(1), 210–230.

Constantinides, E., & Zinck Stagno, M. (2012). Higher education marketing: A study on the impact of social media on study selection and university choice. *International Journal of Technology and Education Marketing*, 2(1), 41–58.

Davis III, C. H., Deil-Amen, R., Rios-Aguilar, C., & Gonzalez Canche, M. S. (2012). *Social media in higher education: A literature review and research directions*. Available at http://www.academia.edu/1220569/Social_Media_in_Higher_Education_A_Literature_Review_and_Research_Directions

Duggan, M., & Brenner, J. (2013). *The demographics of social media users, 2012* (Vol. 14). Washington, DC: Pew Research Center's Internet & American Life Project.

Grimmelmann, J. (2009). Facebook and the social dynamics of privacy. *Iowa Law Review, 95*(4).

Hayes, T. J., Ruschman, D., & Walker, M. M. (2009). Social networking as an admission tool: A case study in success. *Journal of Marketing for Higher Education, 19*(2), 109–124.

JISC. (2011). *Facing up to Facebook: A guide for FE and HE.* Strathclyde, JISClegal.

Kelly, B. (2014). Facebook usage for Russell Group universities. *UK Web Focus: Innovation and best practices for the Web* http://ukwebfocus.wordpress.com/category/social-networking/facebook/. Accessed 27 October 2014.

Kent, M., & Leaver, T. (Eds.). (2014). *An education in Facebook?: Higher education and the world's largest social network.* New York: Routledge.

Madge, C., Meek, J., Wellens, J., & Hooley, T. (2009). Facebook, social integration and informal learning at university: "It is more for socialising and talking to friends about work than for actually doing work". *Learning, Media and Technology, 34*(2), 141–155.

McLoughlin, C., & Lee, M. J. (2014). Beyond friending: Psychosocial engagement on Facebook and its implications for academic success. In M. Kent & T. Leaver (Eds.), *An education in Facebook?: Higher education and the world's largest social network.* New York: Routledge.

Parry, M. (2011). Harvard researchers accused of breaching students' privacy. *The Chronicle of Higher Education.* Available at http://chronicle.com/article/Harvards-Privacy-Meltdown/128166/

Pearce, N. (2010). *Facebook pages in HE.* Digital Scholar http://digitalscholar.wordpress.com/2010/08/27/facebook-pages-in-he/. Accessed 27 October 2014.

Rainie, L., Smith, A., & Duggan, M. (2013). *Coming and going on Facebook:* Pew Internet Project. Available at http://www.pewinternet.org/2013/02/05/coming-and-going-on-facebook/

Stirling, E. (2014). "We use Facebook chat in lectures of course!": Exploring the use of a Facebook group by first-year undergraduate students for social and academic support. In M. Kent & T. Leaver (Eds.), *An education in Facebook?: Higher education and the world's largest social network.* London: Routledge.

Thelwall, M. (2008). Bibliometrics to webometrics. *Journal of Information Science, 34*(4), 605–621.

Wandel, T. (2008). Colleges and universities want to be your friend: Communicating via online social networking. *Planning for Higher Education, 37*(1), 35–48.

Zimmer, M. (2010). "But the data is already public": On the ethics of research in Facebook. *Ethics and Information Technology, 12*(4), 313–325.

CHAPTER 8

Engendering an Online Community: Supporting Students on the Transition into University Life

Sam J. Nolan, Megan Bruce, and Steve Leech

INTRODUCTION

The story begins with the need to support our students. Durham University's Foundation Centre allows direct progression to degrees in all departments for students from non-traditional backgrounds. The student cohort is made up of two main groups: mature local students returning to education and younger international students. Students are supported throughout their learning and prepared to begin Level 1 study in all departments of the University. Through detailed focus groups on the student experience, an issue common to both local and international students was identified. Students felt that after accepting an offer from the University, they "want to start straight away" and "have to wait

---

S.J. Nolan (✉)
Centre for Academic, Researcher and Organisation Development, Durham University, Durham DH1 3LE, UK

M. Bruce • S. Leech
Foundation Centre, University of Durham, Pelaw House, Leazes Road, Durham DH1 1TA, UK

© The Editor(s) (if applicable) and The Author(s) 2016
C.A. Marshall et al. (eds.), *Widening Participation, Higher Education and Non-Traditional Students*,
DOI 10.1057/978-1-349-94969-4_8

forever" to start learning. They often commented on feeling "ignored" and wondered whether they were "the only one" studying subject X at the Foundation Centre. Added to this, foundation students have, perhaps, more barriers to overcome on their path to learning than any other student group. The local mature student cohort is highly motivated, yet for many, the transition into university life represents something of a culture shock. A similar shock occurs with younger international students, many of whom are relocating abroad, learning in a second language for the first time and extending their knowledge. Given the importance of supporting students making the transition into the University, a solution was sought which would engender a sense of community amongst them prior to arriving in Durham. In this chapter, we will describe the evolution of this project. First, we look at background studies on the importance of successful student transition. We then move on to a non-exhaustive review of the reasons for pre-arrival intervention and the current provision, both within the University and across similar higher education institutions (HEIs) in the sector, before introducing this project, its outputs, its successes and the direction of future work in this area.

Pre-arrival: The Critical Phase

For all students the transition into university life is a complex one, as they step away from the known and familiar and enter a new phase of their lives. Keenan (2012), who developed a series of case studies on pre-arrival provision, found that the students' engagement during the pre-arrival stage can be crucial to their subsequent perseverance and success. Moreover, those who fail to engage are more likely to drop out in their first year. On an emotional level, this step into the unknown can be both exciting and frightening in equal measure. In a series of focus groups which form part of our work, foundation students often revealed that, prior to arrival, they thought that they would be "the odd one out," or the only mature/international student, which is rarely the case. In a review of student retention for the Higher Education Academy (HEA), Thomas (2012) found that a sense of belonging to a university was central to retention and success, and this can be fostered through activities which all students engage with. He identifies that student belonging is achieved through:

- supportive peer relations;
- meaningful interaction between staff and students;

- developing knowledge, confidence and identity as successful HE learners;
- an HE experience relevant to students' interests and future goals.
- (Thomas, 2012)

The collegiate system and academic departments at Durham University have a successful track record in supporting students when they start their degree study, but, as noted, and with particular reference to foundation students, pre-arrival support is a key area that can be overlooked. However, as Yorke and Thomas (2003) note, the way a university introduces students from lower socio-economic groups to university life is crucial in enhancing retention and fostering engagement.

Due to the nature of the Foundation Centre cohort, the majority of our students have particular concerns about starting a degree course at a UK HEI. Those who are mature learners may have had a negative experience of education previously which led them to drop out of study, while those who are international are often concerned about the linguistic or cultural aspects of the experience. Lumsden, Mcbryde-Wilding, and Rose (2010) point out that a mismatch between previous educational experience and the differing demands of university expectations is often at the heart of why students tend to be unsuccessful in transitioning to university life. They cite examples such as poor IT skills, lack of analytical reading skills, lack of research skills, and focus on structured learning to pass exams to explain students' lack of success. In addition, research shows that the majority of students who drop out of university do so in the first year. Most of these students cite "lack of preparation for and understanding of the type of learning that is required" (Wingate, 2007, p. 392, in Lumsden et al., 2010). In contrast, students who are most likely to succeed are ones who are embedded from both an academic and social aspect (Lumsden et al., 2010; Wingate, 2007; Reason, Terenzini, & Domingo, 2006; Mayhew, Vanderlinden, & Kyung Kim, 2010).

Our pre-arrival site addresses both of these issues: it has a strong focus on skills required for higher education (HE) in general as well as in specific terms; and it fosters crucial social relationships to allow students to feel connected with one another. Many of our mature students tend not to live in college, so can find it difficult to make friends and connect with other students. Engaging online in discussion fora allows them to build relationships before arriving and makes them feel part of the community before the course begins.

Bain describes university as "one continuous classroom without walls," and pre-arrival engagement underpins this shift in outlook (2012). He argues that every conversation that students have and all the interactions with peers and staff and everything they read contribute to their learning and thinking skills. Facilitating these kinds of interactions with other students and staff for an additional period before the start of the course helps students to make that adjustment earlier than previously possible in their learning journey. In this way, students are able to maximise learning opportunities from the very first day of the face-to-face delivery of the degree programme.

Lumsden et al. (2010) argue that for students entering HE through the non-traditional agenda to be successful there needs to be a shift in understanding of transition. They suggest that resources need to focus on the transition process in the expectation that both learning and retention will be better.

Given the solid background of research others have undertaken in this area, we did a quick review of the work done by other HEIs before developing our own, bespoke solution.

REVIEW OF PRE-ARRIVAL PROVISION

Almost every HEI provider has tackled this problem. In a series of case studies from various HEIs, Keenan (2012) describes different approaches with different outcomes (condensed in Table 8.1).

In addition, work at the University of York (Davis 2011), for example, has shown that such approaches can significantly enhance students' perception of belonging to an academic community—even before they arrive at university. This reduces the attrition rate of students who accept an offer but ultimately fail to complete enrolment. Research evidences that this is a particular issue for first-generation students (Jaschik, 2014). The need for pre-arrival courses has also been noted by both massive open online courses (MOOCs) and commercial course providers. For example, the UK MOOC provider FutureLearn (2014) ran a course, Preparing for Uni (developed and branded for UEA but open to all), which supports students in their transition into HE. Additionally, Palgrave Macmillan—the leading publisher of study skills resources—provides a "Getting ready for academic study" module as part of their *skills4studycampus* pack (Palgrave Macmillan, 2014). Our primary aim in developing a pre-arrival portal

Table 8.1 Summarised from (Keenan, 2012) on the aim and mechanism of online pre-arrival support at several UK HEIs

University	Aim of intervention	Mechanism of intervention
University of Sussex	Direct online registration	Online registration and enrolment web portal
Bournemouth University	Provide contextualized pre-learning activities in a phased manner	VLE based site (*SteppingStones2HE*)
University of Bradford	Engender sense of community amongst incoming students	Social media
Kingston University	Provide concise targeted information and aid in retention	Online pre-arrival portal

for foundation students at Durham was to create a resource tailored to the needs of foundation students which would ease their progress into university life using introductory academic materials. To enhance a feeling of belonging, we also wanted to offer students the opportunity to create an online community through the use of webchats and discussion boards. As has been well documented, students often use social media to communicate pre-arrival (DeAndrea, Ellison, LaRose, Steinfeld, & Fiore, 2012). Our discussion boards were a potentially useful mechanism for allowing students to meet their new classmates.

As has been identified by several authors, both mature students and international students often feel isolated when making the transition into university study. As has been identified by Waller (2006), grouping students as "mature" or "non-traditional" often disguises a vastly diverse set of individuals, each with their own personal set of issues. Waller adds, however, that many mature students feel a sense of social isolation while at university. They often have their own social networks away from their studies and feel isolated from the rest of the student body due to their age. Many studies of international students have discussed several potential barriers they may have to overcome while making the transition into successful study in HE. Andrade (2006) and Mori (2000), for example, both identify language and communication issues and cultural differences as possible barriers. Feelings of isolation and difference affect both mature and international students. Clearly, anything which can alleviate such feelings may ease the progress of students.

Developing a Student-Centred Pre-arrival Platform

To allow use outside the University's virtual learning environment (VLE), we decided to use our own platform to host the pre-arrival portal, this being based on the open source, Drupal CMS. Each student was given a unique username which allowed access to a suite of tailored activities, some specific to their discipline route and some more generic. In addition to allowing us to have control over the look and feel of the site, it allowed for the use of cookies to monitor student use of the various activities. These activities included:

1. Introductory Academic Materials

For each first term module, we produced a short (five minutes) introductory video with the module leader discussing the content, its assessments, and the discipline in general. In some cases, tutors went further and produced additional mini audio and video lectures which introduced key course concepts, previously identified by earlier students as interesting or exciting. In science subjects, students were able to access some of the interactive screen experiments (ISEs) discussed in Chap. 4. As all of our students are entering HE for the first time, the ability to identify with their teachers and become familiar with their teaching style was intended to help to overcome student anxiety.

2. Interviews with Former Students

A series of video interviews with former foundation students were presented, some having just completed the foundation year and others from later in the degree programme. We asked them a series of questions, including:

- Why did you choose to study at Durham University?
  From the students' perspective, this question allowed us to understand what they view as unique, attractive features of the University and its Foundation Centre. A subset of mature students, for instance, felt that the Foundation Centre's position as one of the few direct entry mechanisms to HE at a Russell Group university was an impor-

tant factor for them. Others, many of whose homes were relatively close, were impressed by the range of facilities for mature students.
- Why did you return to education?
  Here we try to ascertain the motivation of the students, their views on the value of learning, and their conceptions about the nature of learning. Many mature students mentioned that recently becoming a parent was a motivating factor, and they suggested that this came from wanting to improve their own situation, but also it would signal the importance of education to their children. Others often discussed dissatisfaction in their current employment and wanting to have a second chance at education.
- Were you made to feel welcome as a mature/international student?
  This question allowed students to explore issues of isolation, and the many different support structures that the Centre, the colleges and the University provide. Both agreed that they were made to feel genuinely welcome and had made fast friends amongst fellow students and staff.
- What is the teaching like?
  Here we got students to explore their perceptions of university classroom learning and the realities of being a member of the Centre. Students often talked about the open nature of the classrooms, where questioning is actively encouraged, and that although many classes were three hours long, a variety of teaching occurred to make the sessions enjoyable.
- How many hours of study are there? How were you able to balance family life and full-time study?
  Given the external demands on many of our mature students, due to family responsibilities, questions on the logistics of daily student learning are important. The approachability of staff was mentioned by one mature student with young children; she found that support and flexibility was important in encouraging her to continue her studies.
- Did you feel well supported at the Foundation Centre?
  Given the significant transitions all our students are undertaking, a supportive environment is crucial. Seeing current students reflect on this is also particularly important. Again, students described the approachability of staff as well as how a community of students, through self-help groups, could provide a lot of additional study group support.

- Did you enjoy your time at the Foundation Centre? Would you recommend the Foundation Centre to a friend?
  These questions pull apart both student enjoyment and their impression that their year of study was worthwhile. All the student volunteers were extremely conscientious and discussed at length their perceptions of the strengths the Centre has. Multiple students commented on the close-knit community of the Centre, and how they had utilised the support of fellow students and staff to develop successful learning practices.
- Did you feel well prepared for undergraduate study?
  Here a former, mature international student (at the time in the second year of a physical sciences degree) discussed how study at the Centre was allowing him to thrive in the later years of his degree.

3. Student Discussion Forum

A discussion board was set up for students to interact with each other. We provided a general discussion space, as well as boards for different clusters of routes (e.g. Science, Social Science, Business, Arts and Humanities). This was a particularly popular element of the site, with over 200 posts in the first year.

4. Live Webchats

Through the month of September (up until the week before students arrive) we ran advertised, scheduled, half-hour webchats using the *Elluminate* platform. These webchats were focussed on the following areas:

- Introduction to the University;
- Introducing the College System;
- Introducing the Foundation Centre;
- Introducing Induction.

The webchats were recorded so that they could be viewed asynchronously. It was noted that around 75% of our new students viewed either the live session or the recording within 48 hours of transmission.

Evaluating the Impact of Our Pre-arrival Portal

1. Student Engagement: Quantitative Measures

In the first year, all elements of the site were available to physical science students, with everything but the introductory academic materials (which were science based) being open to the rest of the student body. In later years, further introductory academic material videos were prepared and all the activities became available to all students. Through tracking web use data, it is clear that student engagement with the site is extremely high, as shown in Figs. 8.1 and 8.2 below:

This evidence and the data from which it is derived indicate that in any given year an average student engages with the site four to five times and typically spends around ten hours on the site pre-arrival. Only around 10% of our students fail to engage with the site at all.

2. Student Engagement: Qualitative Measures

Online feedback was taken from students via the discussion boards, with many elements being positive. For example, "Can't wait to get started—but a bit nervous. I'm also a mature student (30 next year). I have three young children. The website is great too. I've been having a look at the activities and mini lectures—very helpful."

In-depth focus groups revealed that the students often felt isolated over the summer prior to starting with us. As one put it:

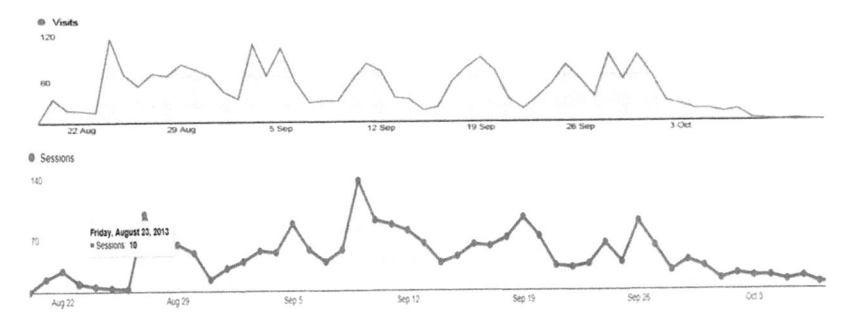

Fig. 8.1 Visits by registered users of the site during summer 2012 (*top*) and 2013 (*bottom*). Weekly peaks can be seen during September as students either watch live or engage with the transmission of each weekly webchat

Fig. 8.2 Integrated visits of registered users to the website during the summers of 2012–2014 by country of users. This indicates significant use by both home mature students and younger international students

> You've accepted an offer, but then it all goes quiet. You just want to get started, but you hear nothing and all the time you're worried about whether you've made the right choice. This website was a godsend, it let you see your tutors, let you talk to your fellow students and with the weekly webchats, made you feel part of something.

Increased student confidence was also evident during the induction week, with students generally aware of where they needed to be, and more engaged with the activities that were taking place. As a staff member put it:

> They often come bounding over and say, I know you'll be teaching me, as I've seen you on the online videos. That initial confidence has really increased, and it allows us to start an effective dialogue around learning earlier.

Supporting Students at a Distance

The item with which students engaged with most over the first two years of the project was the student discussion board. The exchanges were loosely monitored by staff, and their effect is captured by one exchange:

> I'm a little nervous, because I couldn't afford visiting the UK for open campuses, thus I don't know what Durham Uni's atmosphere is like, but I got the feeling that this was one of my biggest and hopefully right decisions to choose this university. Has anyone of you visited Durham Uni? How was it like?

Before staff could reply to reassure the student, one of the prospective, local, mature students responded:

> Hi and welcome. Where abouts in the world are you travelling from? I dont know what Durham uni itself is like but I was born and raised in Durham, so I can assure you, we are a very friendly bunch. :-) (sic)

A friendly dialogue began between the two students. This highlights a key feature of the pre-entry materials: students were encourgaed to work together to support each other. This discussion board offers a mechanism for addressing a key issue in successful transition, a sense of belonging, which can also reduce dropout (Read, Archer, & Leathwood, 2003). This problem can be exacerbated when issues of social and cultural capital can prevent students from feeling a part of the community of the institution. By simply allowing students a mechanism for pre-arrival communication, we help them in overcoming feelings of isolation.

Summary of Key Findings and Future Work

The transition into HE is a difficult time for many incoming freshers and can be even harder for international and mature students, as they enter a new environment, often with a different language and practices to deal with. We were able to develop a successful, pre-arrival online system that built upon examples of good practice, and is being actively used by over 90% of the students.

Following the success of this project, one of the authors (SN) has developed a larger project (Transitions into HE) which was recently funded by the University. Working in partnership with the Careers, Employability and Enterprise Centre at the University, this project will deliver a four-week, online course to all first-year Durham undergraduates in the September prior to their arrival at Durham. The four weeks of the course each address a different issue, namely:

- Preparing for Academic Study

Here, video interviews with current students and staff will show the students' and the tutors' perceptions of the transition into university life.

- Independent Learning

The focus of this unit will be on differences between study at school and at university, with a particular emphasis on the increase in the expected amount of self-directed, independent learning. Activities are being designed which include developing or enhancing time management skills, and on how current students cope with their academic workload, and on developing a work–life balance.

- Digital Literacy and Digital Footprints

This unit will focus on developing skills in using the Internet for academic purposes as well as working in and with library resources to access academic information. A secondary focus will be the use of social media by employers to research prospective job applicants, and on how individual students can manage their own online presence to enhance employability.

- Preparing for Arrival

Finally, this unit, which will be delivered the week prior to arrival, will provide students with both a chance to reflect on the materials covered in the previous units and a look at the significant skill development courses available. In addition, there will be an opportunity for students to ask questions.

Acknowledgements The authors thank Durham University for funding the majority of this work through its Enhancing the Student Learning Experience Award Scheme. Thanks must also go to our summer students Stephen Brayson, Frances Weetman, Jason Hustby and Sarah Learmonth, without whose tireless work this project would not have been possible. Finally, we thank the many tutors and students who gave up their time to take part in interviews.

References

Andrade, M. S. (2006). International students in English-speaking universities: Adjustment factors. *Journal of Research in International Education, 5*(2), 131–154.

Bain, K. (2012). *What the best college students do.* Cambridge: Harvard University Press.

Davis, Simon, Personal communication, 5th January 2011.

DeAndrea, D. C., Ellison, N., LaRose, R., Steinfeld, C., & Fiore, A. (2012). Serious social media: On the use of social media for improving students' adjustment to college. *The Internet and Higher Education, 15*(1), 15–23.

Futurelearn. (2010). Available from: https://www.futurelearn.com/courses/preparing-for-uni/. Last accessed 14 June 2014.

Jaschik, S. (2014). Available from: https://www.insidehighered.com/news/2014/02/17/study-1-hour-program-can-close-achievement-gap-first-generation-college-students. Last accessed 14 June 2014.

Keenan, C. (2012). Pre-arrival: Bizarreness, collisions and adjustments. In M. Morgan (Ed.), *Improving the student experience: A practical guide for universities and colleges.* Abingdon: Routledge.

Lumsden, E., Mcbryde-Wilding, H., & Rose, H. (2010). Collaborative practice in enhancing the first year student experience in higher education. *Enhancing the Learner Experience in Higher Education, 2*(1), 12–24.

Mayhew, M. J., Vanderlinden, K., & Kyung Kim, E. (2010). A multi-level assessment of the impact of orientation programs on student learning. *Research in Higher Education, 51*(4), 320–345.

Mori, S. C. (2000). Addressing the mental health concerns of international students. *Journal of Counselling & Development, 78*(2), 137–144.

Read, B., Archer, L., & Leathwood, C. (2003). Challenging cultures? Student conceptions of 'belonging' and 'isolation' at a post-1992 university. *Studies in Higher Education, 28*(3), 261–277.

Reason, R. D., Terenzini, P., & Domingo, R. J. (2006). First things first: Developing academic competence in the first year of college. *Research in Higher Education, 47*(2), 149–175.

Thomas, L. (2012). *Building student engagement and belonging in higher education at a time of change.* HEA Available at https://www.heacademy.ac.uk/sites/default/files/what_works_summary_report_1.pdf

Waller, R. (2006). 'I don't feel like 'a student', I feel like 'me'!': The oversimplification of mature learners' experience (s). *Research in Post-Compulsory Education, 11*(1), 115–130.

Wingate, U. (2007). A framework for transition: Supporting 'learning to learn' in higher education. *Higher Education Quarterly, 61*(3), 391–405.

Yorke, M., & Thomas, L. (2003). Improving the retention of students from lower socio-economic groups. *Journal of Higher Education Policy and Management, 25*(1), 63–74.

CHAPTER 9

Culture Shock: Applying the Lessons from International Student Acculturation to Non-Traditional Students

Catherine A. Marshall and Jinhua Mathias

INTRODUCTION

As outlined in Chap. 1, there are growing numbers of students from outside the EU accessing HE in the UK and a large number of these students come from China. For a number of reasons, including rapid economic growth, growing study pressure on children in the Chinese education system and the prestige of a Western university degree in the Chinese job market, wealthier Chinese parents are increasingly sending their children abroad to study. The UK is one of the most popular study destinations in Europe, with nearly 90,000 students in 2014. Due to the gap between Chinese high school qualifications and UK university admissions criteria, a one-year foundation programme is often a necessary first step for many Chinese students.

C.A. Marshall (✉) • J. Mathias
Foundation Centre, University of Durham, Pelaw House, Leazes Road, Durham DH1 1TA, UK

© The Editor(s) (if applicable) and The Author(s) 2016
C.A. Marshall et al. (eds.), *Widening Participation, Higher Education and Non-Traditional Students*,
DOI 10.1057/978-1-349-94969-4_9

The issues of educating international students in UK universities have been well studied, with the recognition that there are issues beyond language acquisition affecting learning. There are many cultural differences which, when handled well, can enrich the learning experience for everyone, but which can also lead to tensions and resistance to learning.

Usually when we consider cultural differences, we think of those that arise in distinct countries, encompassing diverse historical, geographical, political, religious and linguistic differences. Yet it is also possible to have different cultures within a country which may be determined by factors such as region and class (Edwards, 1985; Smith, 1991). It would not be unreasonable to expect the diversity of cultures within a country to be represented appropriately in HE; yet in the UK, it is largely the middle classes that use universities, while the working classes are still underrepresented (Archer, Hutchings, & Ross, 2003). The reasons for the low representation of working-class students are likely to be diverse, with economic, social and political issues affecting choices. The cultural differences between social classes with respect to education are also likely to be a reason why students from lower social classes are less likely to be retained (Archer, 2007). It may be possible to use the research on acculturation of international students as a way of supporting non-traditional home students into the HE culture.

Analysis of the research on international student acculturation highlights several areas that may be addressed with respect to working-class students. The identity that an individual develops depends on upbringing and the cultural context of that upbringing; this will affect the individual's attitude towards education, their language and their conceptual organisation. These differences are likely to produce some degree of "culture shock" when that individual moves into a new environment and different cultural norms apply. The process of acculturation has been well documented and includes a set of stages through which an individual passes. If it is possible to recognise these aspects in non-traditional home students, it may be possible to offer explicit support to smooth their transition into HE.

This chapter explores some of these ideas around acculturation, using illustrative quotations from two studies which were conducted to explore the experiences of non-traditional, home students and international students, especially Chinese students, studying on a foundation programme. The information about the experiences of non-traditional students comes from one-to-one interviews conducted with three students who were local, working-class students but of different ages and both sexes. Student A was a 25-year-old female student who left school with no qualifications. Student B was a 50-year-old male student who completed his education at 16 and then went into heavy industry, and Student C is a 49-year-old female who left school at 16. The interviews were conducted in the year following the students' foundation year. They lasted for about an hour, and the questions asked were open to allow the students the opportunity to express their own views and feelings.

The information on international students comes from a study which involved 22 students (numbered 1 to 22) who had left their homes in mainland China for the first time to study a foundation programme in the UK. One focus group, interviews and narrative method were used to explore their learning experience in depth. The interviews were semistructured, students were asked to describe in great detail their daily school life, their various learning approaches and their interaction with teachers and students, both in China and here in the UK. The interviews were audio-recorded, conducted in Chinese and later translated into English, again with the assurance of anonymity. Interviews lasted between 30 and 90 minutes.

Within Chinese culture, the development of conditions of trust is an important prerequisite for achieving openness in any social interaction (Farh, Tsui, Xin, & Cheng, 1998). Therefore, it is particularly important to establish personal trust with the participants. This was achieved through various social contacts. The investigator, as a Chinese speaker, also had advantages to set them at ease so they would express their thoughts during the interviews.

Language Acquisition

It is true to say, academic English is no one's first language: both home and international students have to learn how to write academically. Although international students have passed International English Language Testing System (IELTS) exams in order to study in the UK, their writing ability is quite different from what is required for writing academically. They struggle with both lack of enough vocabulary and knowledge of the structure of English academic writing, which is very different from Chinese writing. For example, Chinese students seem to have a preference for verbal or grammatical parallelism in their English writing to create a symmetrical and harmonious writing structure (Kirkpatrick, 1997). This is because this style of writing is believed to be good Chinese writing. A student did not understand why his English writing was not good when he finished his essay with grammatical parallelism.

> I have won many prizes in Chinese writing. (Student 22)

It is not surprising that writing an essay is an enormous challenge to Chinese students (Murphy, 2011); therefore it is understandable that they easily get stressed when an essay is set.

> Every time there is an essay I felt there is something in my heart; I start to worry about it. (Student 3)

As Murphy (2011) found, citation, reference and avoiding plagiarism are perceived to be significant barriers for Chinese students. Chinese students were accustomed to quoting famous scholars without referencing, assuming everyone knows to whom they are referring. One student argued about plagiarism.

> Teacher says every thought is from somewhere such as books or outside sources and we should reference it, but if it is a very simple and obvious thought, how do I reference it? (Student 4)

Lack of familiarity with the language can also affect how international students interact in the classroom situation. Western educators frequently misjudge how challenging it is to join a class discussion and Chinese students are perceived by Western educators to be very shy in class. The study found that it may be due to many reasons, including language inefficiency, inherited habit from the Chinese classroom, unfamiliarity with Western educational context and culture, and the need to avoid losing face (Mathias, Bruce, & Newton, 2013). Some students find the inability to engage to be frustrating:

> In one class I just prepared an answer but those foreigners (home student) have already answered the question. (Student 7)

The non-traditional home students also expressed some level of difficulty with the language they needed to use at university. Student A describes how she found the transition to using academic English:

> Hard. I don't know big words, I'll try my hardest and I. . . I really cannot just think of a word, but as soon as I've wrote it I think of something. I need to really catch up on my reading a lot, I haven't read hardly anything and that is because of the amount of stress I've had on me. (Student A)

There is also the same resistance, at times, to conforming to the appropriate style and format.

> I was either saying something or I'd written something down and she [the tutor] said, "Yeah, yeah, very good, but you've got to use the right terminology." But why, if I'm saying the right things, does it matter, and she said, "Oh yes, it does." So remembering the right terminology is very difficult. (Student B)

Language is intimately connected to development of identity; it provides visible and audible boundaries and it provides members of a group with a means of sharing and agreeing upon distinctive principles and values (Byram, 1992). It may be considered that non-traditional home students and international students are very different when it comes to their language needs. For the home students English is their first language, however, it is somewhat more nuanced than that as there are different ways in which language is spoken within a country, with clear divisions of acceptability.

Edwards states that "the possession of a given language is well-nigh essential to the maintenance of group identity" (1985, p. 3). He goes on to discuss attitudes towards dialect and he explains that there is no aesthetic or linguistic basis for superiority or inferiority of dialects; it depends on which group is in power. Despite this he notes that "Dialect has long been used, of course, to denote a substandard deviation from some prestigious variety or standard form" (1985, p. 21).

Bourdieu notes that students who use articulate and varied language may be perceived as being innately more intelligent, when their language is likely to be highly dependent on cultural capital (1976). To some degree it can be argued that the non-traditional students have to learn academic English as distinct from the dialect they grew up with. Student B also describes how he found it a struggle but how he expects the new language to become more natural in the way that Berger and Luckmann (1966) describe how students learning a second language take time before the new language develops reality and can be used without referral back to the mother tongue:

> Obviously things are sticking in my head otherwise I wouldn't be able to do the essays properly, I wouldn't be getting decent marks, so things are sticking in, it just seems hard work all the time remembering the correct terminology; how to write an essay and citations and all that. Because they're all new and anything that you do that's new takes time to sink in. I'm just hoping that next year and the year after it will become habit. (Student B)

LANGUAGE AND CONCEPTUAL ORGANISATION

In addition to language being important in the development of identity, it also determines how we develop our conceptual organisation (Lantolf, 1999). In Lantolf's discussion of concept acquisition and how culture determines the way in which we organise our minds, he looks at the work of Vyotsky and how the development of conceptual thinking in childhood leads to concept of self. "It is in dialogues that children appropriate the words of others through listening to others speak to them, and in so doing appropriate the organizational patterns (concepts) of the culture, including a concept of self" (1999, p. 35). Words take on layers of meaning depending on culture; so definitions of words from a dictionary sense may be more limited than the way they are used in language.

There was no scope in these small projects to meaningfully explore differences in conceptual organisation; however, both home and international students were able to articulate some changes to the ways in which they were thinking and expressing themselves:

> I wrote about this maths game, to do with logic and I said that I thought it was a logical teaching tool and I was quite amazed because the way I speak didn't actually marry up with the way I write. I'm coming out with all these words and I write this essay and I'm amazed I wrote that because it's not how I speak at all. (Student C)

> When you learn something you understand it by thinking through it, once you understand it you don't need to memorise it because it is dissolved into your blood (融化到血液中). It turns a very natural thing to you. (Student 17)

> I think more independently, not like before just relying on the teacher. (Student 5)

> It is more like a research, using more brain, spending more time thinking. (Student 3)

Cultural Attitudes Towards Education

It may be that some of the differences in socioeconomic group representation in the UK HE system are due to differing cultural attitudes inculcated by habitus towards education. As described earlier, Bourdieu's model of outlining the role of education in reproducing the social class system may explain why children from lower social classes do not always benefit from compulsory education as much as children from higher social classes. At this stage of education, the children have no choice about participating, but once past the age of compulsory education, other aspects of cultural alienation may be apparent in the choices they make about participation.

For students from lower socio-economic backgrounds, the culture that they experience as they grow up is formative in respect of their identity, language and conceptual processes. The education that they experience is largely directed at the middle classes and values middle-class culture and language rather than the one with which they are familiar (Archer, 2007). Consequently, when students from lower socio-economic class enter university, they do not have the cultural capital that middle-class students have and are likely to develop a different learner identity compared to students from more advantaged backgrounds (Marshall, 2013).

> No one's like me, no one's like from my way, none of them, they're all better they're all nicer and you can trust them. (Student A)

Chinese students have a similar experience; they feel different and they feel lonely, finding it difficult to be in the inner circle of English students.

> Normally we have a good time with English students, some are nice but I feel it is difficult to get involved, maybe my English is not good enough. (Student 3)

> Even though you may have a few (English) friends, it is still difficult for you to be truly immersed in (the English circle of friends). Because, in the UK, if you cannot drink, and do not have a girlfriend, you are very lonely. (Student 9)

These identity differences are likely to produce a level of "culture shock" when an individual moves into a different cultural arena, for example, a student coming to HE from a family and school with no tradition of HE. There will then be a process of acculturation, which has a set of stages through which an individual passes which are likely to mirror those of international students (Marshall, 2013).

According to Cushner (1994), the issue of belonging is important. Exclusion leads to individuals experiencing feelings of loneliness, alienation, loss of self-esteem as well as developing a decreased sense of direction. If students are to be in a position to gain the most from their educational experiences, they need to feel engaged and included in the process. It is important that the teachers are aware of the impact of verbal and non-verbal forms of communication and that there are different styles based on gender, culture and so on (Cushner, 1994). The process of cross-cultural adaptation is dynamic and stressful and can be seen as a cycle of experiencing new situations, which the student finds stressful, leading to a withdrawal from the process and then a readjustment to adapt to the new situation (Kim, 1988).

Certainly, coming to university is likely to be a change for all students. Whereas a traditional 18-year-old student will be dealing with new experiences of living independently, the local, working-class student and the international student will be adapting to a new language and new ways of communicating and thinking.

None of the home students interviewed felt that their families even considered university as an option and they were not expected to continue their education past the age of 16. Student B explains that his family were concerned for him to be happy and healthy as he grew up, but he was expected to leave school and go out to work at 16.

> So I went straight from there [school] to heavy industry. I served my time in an apprenticeship as a boiler-maker and plater. The job was already there, before I left school, it's like this old boys' network, in the working men's club and my dad knew the guy that was doing the interview: "Not a problem, Leo, the job's already there for him." (Student B)

Neither Student A nor Student B felt that there were any teachers at school who had their interests at heart; in fact, Student B remembers being regularly caned at school, and on coming top of the class in Maths, was told by his teacher that it would not do him any good. Student A says that the teachers meant "nothing at all" to her:

> To tell you the truth the teachers didn't care, they really taught you nothing. When I first started school I was dead excited and especially in sciences,

> I used to love chemistry and stuff like that but then you'd ask some questions and they'd make you feel stupid for asking and stuff like that so in the end you'd just mess on and not be bothered. (Student A)

This contrasted strongly with the expectations of the international students' families. The decision to study abroad may be initiated either by students or by parents, but as most international students tend to be economically dependent, it is generally made jointly with parents. In the survey of foundation Chinese students, more than 90% stated that the decision to study at Durham University was a joint decision with their parents. Therefore, international students are well supported by their family financially and emotionally.

On the other hand, good financial support also means high expectation from parents. Due to the high cost of education abroad, parents of international students expect them to do well to achieve a degree which can secure their future career. Bodycott and Lai studied the influence and implications of Chinese culture in the decision to undertake cross-border HE, and claimed, "The influence of these parents extends beyond initial decision making and impacts on the student's social and academic well-being." (2012, p. 252). When interviewing Chinese students, it was found that often a common question that the parents ask their children abroad on telephone is about study. A student had to change her degree from media study to law because her parents believe that this provides her a better career.

The learning environment the students find themselves in is also likely to be more different from their previous experiences than traditional UK A level students. For the international students the cultural difference to education is caused by geographical distance, whereas for the mature, non-traditional home students the difference is caused by temporal distance:

> So it was the learning aspect, because I hadn't been in an education environment for a long, long time. So I thought that would be very difficult getting back into the routine of taking notes, being able to read my notes, listen to what people are saying, taking the information in and trying to retain it. I thought that would be the biggest stumbling block…the lecturers were different to what I expected; maybe, an us and them lecturer and pupil type of thing exactly as it was at school. Because that's the only learning environment I've been in. You know the teachers stood there and told you what to do: "Take your coats off, blah, blah, blah, blah." It was totally different, it was as if the lecturers wanted you to do well… It was very interactive so it was different from the learning environment that I knew. (Student B)

The interactive style was also very different for the Chinese students:

> I am used to be quiet in class; in China we never voluntarily answer questions. It is showing off. How can you expect us to change the habit in such a short time? Now I start to get used to it but it takes time. I must get used to it because there are often discussions, I have no choice. I feel I have made progress. (Student 1)

There were Chinese students who liked the interactive teaching style:

> I did not like maths in China; it was too fast. I did not understand in class and did not have time to ask the teacher; I was gradually lagging behind. Here you learn and then practise and ask in class. I enjoy it much more now. (Student 10)

> It is not like you are thinking on your own; we share ideas and more ideas come out through discussion and the brain works faster. So you don't feel nervous, it is fun especially when there is a competition, like playing a game. (Student 2)

It can be said that the most difficult academic challenge for many international students who have just left high school is time management. Learning activities are always managed by teachers at school in China and the activities are time-consuming: 12 hours a day and six or seven days a week study compared with less than 20 hours a week organised contact time at a UK university. The unexpected responsibility of managing study on their own makes them feel they are lost. Some motivated students may try to organise time effectively, but as one student commented:

> On many occasions I had nothing to do after coming back to the flat, don't have homework every day; even if there is an assignment, you don't need to finish it until a few weeks later, plus you don't want to start immediately. So (you) have nothing to do. Normally go on to Internet and chat with friends. (Student 2)

Additionally, many Chinese students have no experience of being independent in both living and learning; hence they were shocked initially when they found out that they have to make many decisions and learn by themselves.

> Here the teacher teaches you into a topic but the topic may have many branches so I don't know what to study. (Student 8)

The belief that learning is not just an activity in the classroom but also self-regulated, independent exploration of the knowledge they are interested in without the teacher's guidance is a great challenge. It takes some time for students to appreciate independent learning style, and resistance to independent learning still exists among some students who believe it is not useful for exams.

> Teacher listed reading list but I read none. Even if I read them it won't be in the exam anyway. (Student 7)

The non-traditional students also have time management issues, but in their case it is managing their normal home life alongside the university life:

> The biggest difficulty was time management. I'm not prepared to let anything go but trying to fit everything in. Instead of planning and doing my assignments in the time I've got, I think, "Well, I've got six weeks..." I think I'd better start doing something, at that point the time management I'm finding difficult, but that's purely down to me it's not anything that anyone else can sort out. (Student B)

THE PROCESS OF ACCULTURATION

For the international student, while there is likely to be strong support for their progression to HE, the UK institution in which they find themselves is likely to be different from what they have experienced before and may also be different from HE experiences of members of their family who have not attended a UK institution.

For the traditional student, the move to university is likely to be seen as a natural next step, by themselves and their families, whereas for the local, working-class students they may be stepping outside of the expectations held for them by their families and that they hold about themselves. This can be seen as a form of secondary socialisation. Berger and Luckman describe secondary socialisation as "the internalization of institutional or institution-based 'sub-worlds'" (1966, p. 158). In secondary socialisation, the learning sequences are important in establishing the knowledge that must be acquired to access the new sub-world, although the stipulations of the level of knowledge required may be a further function of an elite group setting barriers rather than a pragmatic approach to the level actually required.

Berger and Luckmann (1966) observe that there is usually some resistance to challenges to the internalisation of socialisation and that the resistance is much greater in respect of primary socialisation than secondary and that secondary socialisation may occur several times.

Often in the classroom, Chinese students have a habit of sitting together, and tutors do not understand how difficult it is to break this habit.

> The biggest challenge is making friends; my close circle of friends are Chinese, then it can be expanded to classmates. In the canteen all the Chinese sit together, all the foreigners sit together. It is just like habit, Chinese people naturally talk when they are together so foreigners may feel they can't chip in, so they don't want to sit with us, but in fact if English people like to sit with us we certainly will speak English. So I think both sides have problems. I really want to join the foreigners' circle but if I join the foreigners' group my relationship with my Chinese friends will be cold so I'd really like all my Chinese friends to mix with English people. But due to the language barrier it is not easy to do this, so it is a very awkward thing. (Student 21)

In his paper on cross-cultural adaptation, Kim (1988) recognises that personality attributes and preparedness for change will affect the rate of adaptation to a new culture, and Byram (1996) noted that some of the attributes likely to support successful acculturation included curiosity, openness, suspension of judgement and the ability to analyse one's own behaviours. This is clearly illustrated in the recognition of behaviours by one Chinese student:

> I know that some students worry about the answer being wrong, so other people might laugh at you, and so you lose face. But in fact once you break this [psychological] barrier you feel ok. If you never want to break this barrier you will never have a chance [to speak]. Some people I know that their English is good but don't dare to speak in class, but they write beautiful English. When they really spoke in class they were good, not like me making a lot of mistakes, even the teacher sometimes doesn't understand me. I feel if you lose face a few times you feel it does not matter anymore. (Student 6)

The difficulties inherent in acculturation mean that students often need support to help them adjust. Tutors on the foundation programme can certainly identify particular times in the term when students are more likely to be feeling "low" about the course before making a readjustment to seeing themselves as students again. For example, by Week 5 of the first term, many of the students are facing in-class tests and are writing assignments to hand in. These are new experiences to many of them and the stress causes some students to question why they are on the course and to consider dropping out. With support and encouragement, most of them stay on, and when they start to get results back from the tests and assignments, the morale improves again. In the following extract from one learning log, a non-traditional student describes how she felt each week in one module. There is a new experience of learning the subject which is hard and some withdrawal and even some anger by Week 4. In Week 6, there is evidence of readjustment in the way that she approaches her work, and by Week 8, she is feeling confident.

> Week 1: Nothing went in and I found it so hard to understand.
> Week 2: I researched a lot more for this week's lesson and felt much better.
> Week 3: First part of the lesson went well, but the latter half I lost concentration and struggled.
> Week 4: I emailed the tutor in a panic and he replied he'd talk about the test on Friday. I felt it was another wasted lesson.
> Week 5: I don't think I did very well on the test, but I knew the first few sections.
> Week 6: I did loads of reading before the lesson and wrote notes. It helped so much. I understood everything and left on a positive note.
> Week 8: Got our assignment and can't wait to start! Feeling really confident.

This progress was also noted in the quotations from some of the Chinese students:

> At the beginning I felt it was very difficult to write 1500 words, then later when I was able to write 3000 words essay, 1500 words essay is not a big deal. (Student 4)

Conclusion: Implications for the Foundation Programme

The acquisition of intercultural competence by international students has been studied widely, and Byram (1996) suggests that to encourage the development of cultural competence, the dominant cultural capital should not be the only one transmitted to the learner. The learning environment should also take into account the learner's own cultural background so they are not alienated by that promoted by the educational establishment.

> Of course they [home students] know more than us because it is about English history. Even for the topic about World War II, it is from English point of view, we have no knowledge of it. (Student 4)

A study by Hockings, Cooke and Bowl shows that non-traditional students want "to be recognised and respected as people with something to offer" (2007, p. 721), yet students from working-class backgrounds often feel alienated by the dominant culture, particularly in elite universities. Cushner agrees that sociocultural inclusion is important in successfully teaching a diverse group of students and makes suggestions on how to achieve this. The curriculum should be inclusive and "focus on all students and integrate the contributions of many different people and groups to the history and experiences of a nation and the world" (1994, p. 121). A wide range of teaching strategies should be employed and methods of assessment should be varied, for example, the use of portfolios can be a supportive method of assessment. However, the dominant pedagogy in HE remains the lecture, particularly as student numbers have increased, and the dominant assessment method is the examination (Hockings, Cooke, & Bowl, 2007).

The foundation programme has attempted to adopt an inclusive pedagogic style, which focuses on student interaction. Students are taught in classes of up to 30 students, and the mixed methods include lectures, workshops, discussions, practical work, field trips and group work. The curriculum has been designed to be as inclusive as possible while still preparing students for the progression route they have chosen. For example, the module "Cultural Studies" allows students to view their own culture alongside those of others and to recognise and value that culture. Assessment does include examinations, as this will be the main assessment method in the subsequent years of their degrees, but portfolio work is also used, as well as essays, presentations, posters, and other forms of continuous assessment. Attention is focussed on language: students take study skills modules, which help them learn to write in an academic style, and the specialised vocabulary for subjects is taught explicitly. For example, in the first biology module that students take, the notes accompanying the module include glossaries for each section. The specialist vocabulary is also made available in advance of the lecture using the virtual learning environment Durham University On-line (DUO), to enable students to prepare for the lecture.

Our studies indicated that both non-traditional home students and Chinese international students actively adopt those new learning strategies which help their understanding; for example, they enjoy doing experiments, make an effort to take part in verbal discussion and learn to think critically. They strive to be competent learners and therefore are willing to risk taking on the emotional challenge of moving outside their "zone of comfort" in order to adapt to the UK HE learning style. The studies also indicate that they are reflective learners, willing to accept their own responsibilities, and many of them have realised the importance of time management and independent study. However, adjustment to this learning style is not uniform. Anecdotal evidence shows that those more mature and intrinsically motivated students seemed to fully appreciate the benefit of the learning styles promoted in the foundation course while others still have difficulties in particular with time management and independent learning; hence, more support and guidance would be needed to help them develop learning autonomy. This should not be a surprise because to develop self-regulated learning and intellectual capacity of university students has always been the focus of HE in Western universities (Entwistle, 2000).

There are clear parallels to be drawn between the acculturation that international students undergo when they enter university and the adaptations that non-traditional students make in an elite university. If a university wishes to improve its teaching of international students, it is necessary to empower lecturers with knowledge concerning cultural learning style. Good teaching in an international context should be culturally inclusive and language-level appropriate, often requiring simple modifications such as the need for slow-paced teaching, giving unambiguous instructions, using cross-cultural examples and increasing thinking time. A good teacher should be not only enthusiastic about her or his subject but also have ability to make a good rapport so as to manage a culturally diverse group. To help students' adjustment, academic tutors should be aware of the challenges students face in the specific context, such as problems students may encounter during induction, time management, self-regulated learning skill.

There is some evidence that the foundation programme works for those students who have the right attributes to enable them to adapt and move into a new culture, particularly those who are older and have more experience of secondary socialisation. If the programme is to be successful with younger, less self-confident students, more adaptation of the pedagogic styles may be necessary, not just within the programme, but at all levels through the University.

It can be argued that this diversity of approach will enrich the academic community; students were able to clearly articulate that they valued being part of a diverse community:

> In group discussion, those UK mature students just like teachers, they take responsibility to explain to you things, I felt I understood better in the group. (Student 7)

While one of the non-traditional students explains why she enjoys mixing with a diverse group of students at university:

> I like the people… they've got interesting things to say to you. Whereas the people round our way, the only thing they've got to talk about is what the next-door neighbours did last night. (Student A)

References

Archer, L. (2007). Diversity, equality and higher education: A critical reflection on the ab/uses of equity discourse within widening participation. *Teaching in Higher Education, 12*, 635–653. doi:10.1080/13562510701595325.

Archer, L., Hutchings, M., & Ross, A. (2003). *Higher education and social class: Issues of exclusion and inclusion.* Abingdon: RoutledgeFalmer.

Berger, P., & Luckmann, T. (1966). *The social construction of reality.* Harmondsworth: Penguin.

Bodycott, P., & Lai, A. (2012). The influence and implications of Chinese culture in the decision to undertake cross-border higher education. *Journal of Studies in International Education, 16*(3), 252–270. doi:10.1177/1028315311418517.

Bourdieu, P. (1976). The school as a conservative force: Scholastic and cultural inequalities. In R. Dale, G. Esland, & M. MacDonald (Eds.), *Schooling and capitalism.* London: Routledge/Keegan Paul in association with the Open University.

Byram, M. (1992). Foreign language learning for 'European citizenship'. *Language Learning Journal, 6*, 10–12.

Byram, M. (1996). Describing intercultural communication and the 'intercultural speaker'. *Paper presented at the National Foreign Language Centre,* Washington, DC.

Cushner, K. (1994). Preparing teachers for an intercultural context. In R. W. Brislin & T. Yoshida (Eds.), *Improving intercultural interactions. Modules for cross-cultural training programmes* (pp. 109–128). London: Sage.

Edwards, J. (1985). *Language, society and identity*. Oxford: Blackwell.

Entwistle, N. J. (2000). Approaches to studying and levels of understanding: The influences of teaching and assessment in higher education. In J. C. Smart (Ed.), *Handbook of theory and practice* (Vol. X, pp. 156–218). New York: Agathon Press.

Farh, J., Tsui, A. S., Xin, K., & Cheng, B. (1998). The influence of relational demography and guanxi: The Chinese case. *Organization Science, 9*(4), 471–488.

Hockings, C., Cooke, S., & Bowl, M. (2007). 'Academic engagement' within a widening participation context: A 3D analysis. *Teaching in Higher Education, 12*, 721–733. doi:10.1080/13562510701596323.

Kim, Y. Y. (1988). *Communication and cross-cultural adaptation: An integrative theory*. Clevedon: Multilingual Matters.

Kirkpatrick, A. (1997). Traditional Chinese text structures and their influence on the writing in Chinese and English of contemporary mainland Chinese students. *Journal of Second Language Writing, 6*(3), 223–244. doi:10.1016/S1060-3743(97)90013-8.

Lantolf, J. P. (1999). Second culture acquisition. In Hinkel (Ed.), *Culture in second language teaching and learning*. Cambridge: Cambridge University Press.

Marshall, C. A. (2013). True internationalisation: Lessons from the IFP classroom for widening participation. *InForm, 11*, 11–13.

Mathias, J., Bruce, M., & Newton, D. P. (2013). Challenging the Western stereotype: Do Chinese international foundation students learn by rote? *Research in Post-Compulsory Education, 18*(3), 221–238.

Murphy, P. (2011). Raising awareness of the barriers facing international students in the UK and the need for two-way adaption. *Paper presented at the Internationalisation of Pedagogy and Curriculum in Higher Education Conference*, University of Warwick.

Smith, A. D. (1991). *National identity*. Harmondsworth: Penguin.

CHAPTER 10

Adjusting Teaching Practices for Mature Adults to Incorporate Understandings of Affective Processes and Self-efficacy in Maths

Mary D. Dodd

AFFECTIVE ISSUES

Since the early work by Tobias and Buxton (1981) on maths anxiety, considerable research has taken place on adults' responses towards maths. Early work was somewhat anecdotal, but descriptions of behaviours which might be symptoms of anxiety such as Bibby's (2002) passing and self-denigration have found real resonance with the experience of many maths educators, and the notion that maths can engender strong emotions in people, both positive and negative, is now firmly embedded in adult education.

Buxton (1981) particularly identified severe anxiety, which he labelled as panic. Other studies have since identified a range of emotions such as shame (Bibby, 2002), and indeed, interviews with foundation students

M.D. Dodd (✉)
Foundation Centre, University of Durham, Pelaw House, Leazes Road, Durham
DH1 1TA, UK

(Dodd, 2012) have included mention of lack of confidence, anxiety, fear and guilt. For example:

> I was very, quite anxious about it at the beginning of the year and was thinking, maths, I won't be able to do it.

and from another student:

> I always felt awful when my kids were growing up because I couldn't help them.
> (Dodd, 2012, p. 281)

Many examples in literature focus on small intervention projects for people with self-confessed maths anxiety, and hence, I would argue against the overgeneralisation that all adults are anxious about maths or dislike challenge. Research on adults' maths memories by Karsenty (2004), for example, indicated a more diverse range of views. She was able to classify her participants' views of maths into five categories, only one of which indicated anxiety. The other four were exciting and enjoyable, challenging but manageable, unimportant and generating indifference and general lack of interest in any school learning.

More recently, Klinger (2007) investigated anxiety and attitudes of Foundation and Access students in comparison with undergraduate students (248 valid responses), using detailed factor analysis to consider potential influences of gender, schooling and so on. He confirmed that, as he had expected, levels of maths anxiety and negative attitudes were higher for women than for men, for those enrolled on arts and humanities courses than on science courses and for those educationally disadvantaged (i.e. many Foundation/Access students).

When Durham University foundation students were asked to rate their anxiety levels about future study and future maths study on a scale of 1 to 10 (Fig. 10.1), it was found that, in general, more students were anxious about maths than their overall study, some giving as much as six rankings difference. These results support the claim that some students might have high levels of anxiety, although clearly some do not.

Whilst some students are happy to admit anxiety or previous issues with maths, others are less willing to acknowledge or explore this area. One group that sometimes causes particular difficulty for teaching is the people who have managed a Maths General Certificate of Secondary Education

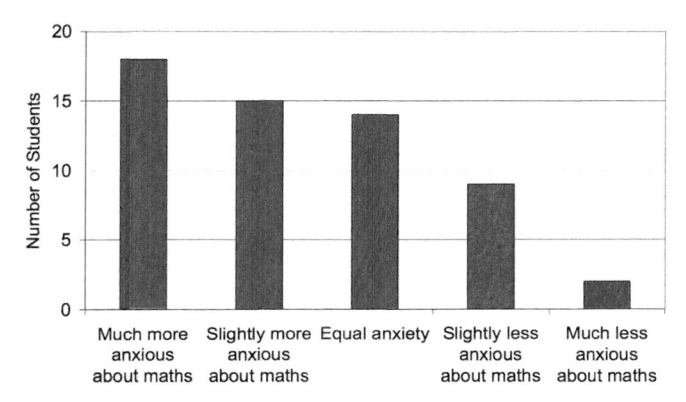

[Bar chart: Number of Students by anxiety category — Much more anxious about maths: 18; Slightly more anxious about maths: 15; Equal anxiety: 14; Slightly less anxious about maths: 9; Much less anxious about maths: 2]

Fig. 10.1 Comparison of anxiety about maths study with anxiety about foundation study in general (Home students Oct 2007)

(GCSE) and gained the associated recognition of being "successful at maths" but whose apparent success masks only limited understanding. Some students may be happy to acknowledge this potential weakness: "I don't know how I managed it!" or believe that previous success represented a pinnacle in their achievement which has since deteriorated: "I was better at maths then!" However, others do not wish to acknowledge concerns with their understanding, perhaps even to themselves. I have labelled this group, "fragile achievers" since, for them, their previous achievement is too fragile to risk damaging. This lack of confidence can manifest itself in a range of actions designed to hide uncertainties both from themselves and others. These might include diverting attention from areas of weakness by asking obscure questions, "helping" a student who is finding difficulty by showing a "superior method" to the tutor, avoiding revisiting certain topics for fear of identifying something is no longer understood or an unwillingness to engage with new methods for fear they may destabilise previous learning.

Many writers (Bibby, 2002; Buxton, 1981; Safford, 2000; Walen & Williams, 2002) suggest that there is often a negative correlation between anxiety and achievement, although as Evans (2000) points out, this view of anxiety interfering with performance is a dominant view but not the only one. He describes an alternative view, where low levels of anxiety actually improve performance with some optimum level of anxiety maximising success. When foundation students completed a series of maths questions at the start of their course and were asked to indicate their level of anxiety, no clear correlation could be seen between anxiety and performance (Dodd, 2012). However, as Fig. 10.2 shows, all students who identified themselves as "not at all anxious" gained high marks.

Those gaining the lowest marks identified themselves as "very anxious" but it cannot be distinguished from these results alone whether it was the anxiety that caused the low performance as in a Buxton (1981) panic type reaction or whether it was lack of mathematical skill that caused the low performance and it was an awareness of this lack that caused the anxiety. It should not be assumed that those identified as anxious always do badly; some of those labelled as "very anxious" actually performed very well, supporting Evans's (2000) suggestion that anxiety might sometimes improve performance.

BELIEF AND ATTITUDE

Two further ideas—negative self-image (Duffin & Simpson, 2000; Karsenty, 2004; Klinger, 2007) and low levels of self-efficacy (Bandura, 1994; Safford, 2000)—are of particular interest for foundation teaching practice because they have the potential to be most readily changed.

Bandura (1994) used the term "self-efficacy" to describe people's judgement or belief in their own competencies. Crucially, he showed that perceived levels of self-efficacy contributed to motivation, perfor-

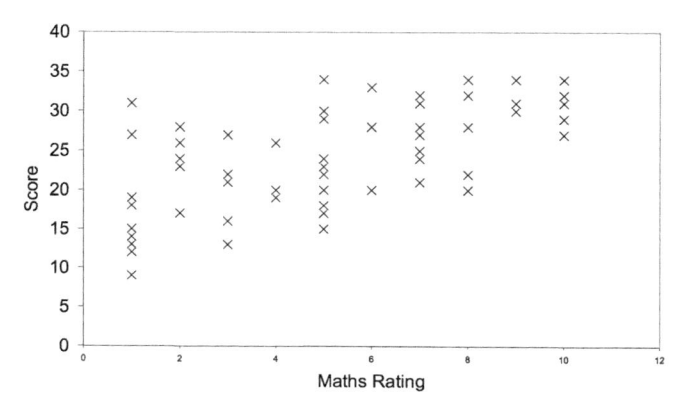

Fig. 10.2 A scattergram to compare scores with maths anxiety rating (Home students 2007)

mance and, hence, achievement. Thus, adult teaching practices that focus on improving self-efficacy could, ultimately, improve learning. Bandura (1994) suggested that self-efficacy was influenced by experiences of success and failure. Hence, structuring adult teaching to maximise opportunities for success, mitigating any previous school experiences, would lead to improvement. There are of course many ways to structure adult teaching to achieve this.

In Durham University's Foundation Centre, worksheets are designed with a dual purpose, not only to ensure that the requisite sub-skills are mastered but also to provide opportunities for students to demonstrate success, thus contributing to the cycle of positive reinforcement and improved self-efficacy. Repetition of similar question types with different numbers provides opportunities to confirm understanding that can immediately be checked with answers. Positive reinforcement is sometimes embraced by students who have been observed to cover their own work with a series of large ticks in red pen, despite the non-use of red pen in tutor marking practices. However, sadly, self-denigration in the form of large crosses has also been observed.

The most essential part of this structuring of teaching practice is derived from the actions of the teachers themselves. A significant influence of the radical constructivist approach for teaching has been its emphasis on trying to interpret learning construction through the eyes of the learner by imagining how that learner might be viewing the problem. Using the premise that:

> When students genuinely engage in solving mathematical problems, they proceed in personally reasonable and productive ways.
> (Confrey, 1991, p. 111)

work that had previously been just labelled "wrong," or perhaps, worse, "a good try," now becomes something of value to be interpreted. For example, Lannin, Barker, and Townsend (2007) described how students can start with a correct procedure and then make their own adaptations (or "repairs") for a new situation which, although incorrect, may seem sensible to the students. Lannin et al. (2007) referred to this idea as "repair theory."

Attempting to understand students' ways of thinking allows teachers to guide and redirect constructively or to link individual mistakes together for more effective remediation (Confrey, 1991). For a teacher, willingness to listen and to try to interpret other ways of thinking leads to a more empathic approach. For the student, the notion that work is of value to the teacher is labelled as a partial success rather than a failure, leading to empowerment and increased self-efficacy.

The move of adults towards ownership of learning and empowerment (Knowles, 1980) might be influential in reducing the perceived power of previous criticism. There may be a belief that a "past self" might not have been able to do something but, perhaps, a "new self" can. The determination to succeed in itself may be influential in decisions to continue with a task rather than give up, which in turn may lead to success and improved self-efficacy. Bandura (1994) also noted the influence of "social modelling," of people identifying role models and equating their own possibilities of success with the success of their role model, an idea firmly embedded in the use of case studies within Foundation Centre publicity and in decisions to allocate previous successful foundation students as mentors.

In summary then, improving the negative self-image and levels of self-efficacy of adults has the potential to be one of the easiest and most effective ways to improve learning for some adults. Structuring teaching to incorporate experiences of success, encouraging mentoring and role models (Bandura, 1994) and increased determination returning as an adult (Benn, 1997) all have the possibility of raising self-efficacy, and this in turn would increase the motivation, performance and ultimate success of students (Bandura, 1994). The following section gives some examples of ways that this might be done based on practices that have proven beneficial within the Foundation Centre.

Examples of Practice

First Encounter: Making Common Issues Explicit, Removing Feelings of Isolation and Transferring Blame from the Student to Past Circumstances

Group brainstorms on words that come to mind when "maths" is mentioned are usually a successful way to introduce the idea that some people have very negative emotions (but also that some do not). For some people, just the public recognition of such emotions and the discovery that others within the group share them is a major step in removing feelings of isolation. The widespread existence of such feelings can be further emphasised by talking about the regular appearance of some words whenever a similar brainstorm has taken place in the past or the presentation of responses from previous cohort questionnaires. The mention of research literature, for example, Buxton's (1981) work with professional people, Coben's (2000) work on adult life histories and Bibby's (2002) work with primary teachers, can be used to increase the legitimacy about such feelings.

More subtly, the acknowledgement of such information by the tutor highlights the tutor's own awareness of the issues, providing reassurance about future maths study. Feedback responses from Taster days and Admissions Applications from those who have attended Taster days suggest that the use of such activities have been well received and instrumental in providing reassurance for those anxious about maths.

Whether used on a Taster Day or in the first session of teaching, the introductory activity also provides the opportunity to start talking about words such as "guilt" and "shame" (Bibby, 2002) that rarely appear on public brainstorms but frequently appear when students look back (Dodd, 2012). A recognition that people will have forgotten maths, that it is acceptable to not be able to do maths and that others may also be hiding feelings of guilt may act as the first stage in the long process of making "fragile achievers" willing to fully engage.

Discussions about some of the common issues that have triggered maths emotion (Bibby, 2002; Coben, 2000; Karsenty, 2004; Safford, 2000; Sewell, 1981), and particularly the way one "bad" teacher, one poor experience, missing one "vital" maths skill through illness or overpressure from others may have started the problem, begin to shift the blame from the persons themselves to their past experiences, a first step in the process of reducing negative self-image. The success of this process is characterised by this comment from a student at the end of their course:

> I now don't think I'm thick and stupid, I just had a bad teacher.
> (Student comment, Dodd, 2012, p. 294)

Constructive Student–Student and Student–Tutor Interactions

The importance of creating a supportive environment of mutual trust and respect cannot be underestimated. The successful small group intervention projects identified in literature vary considerably in theoretical approach, activity and even beliefs about maths, but all student responses identify the importance of the tutor and value of working with other students. It is only as mutual trust begins to build that people become willing to explore their own mathematical weaknesses, but such actions sometimes require the breaking down of barriers between student and tutor created from years of conditioning. There needs to be a change in student perception of the tutor from "significant other" to learning support. Activities which promote sharing of understandings and scaffolding (Wood, Bruner, & Ross, 1976) between small groups of students are to be encouraged. Activities which reinforce the separation between tutor and student, recreate negative experiences from previous education or highlight differences in understandings between students are to be avoided. The planning of a teaching session using this template immediately calls into question many standard teaching techniques but sometimes these same techniques can be used in a different way to provide a positive effect.

Asking a maths question from the front to an individual is rarely an appropriate action for a group containing people with mixed feelings about maths. If the person answering does not give the correct answer, they are being publicly shamed. The awareness of this possibility, and its occasional deliberate use in school to produce precisely this effect, does not help the person answering to think as clearly as possible even if they had the skill to answer the question. The alternative approach of selecting only a person likely to give the correct answer or the person keen to volunteer an answer is also not appropriate. This emphasises the isolation and feelings of inferiority of the person who cannot answer. A much more successful strategy is to allocate questions to three or four students together and then challenge the answers from other groups. Better yet, asking the group to create the questions for others to answer, especially the tutor, reverses the entire tutor–student relationship whilst deepening understanding at the same time.

The use of voting must be considered carefully. The public presentation of a frequency bar chart from electronic voting which shows 99 people gave the correct answer and only one gave the incorrect answer increases the isolation of the one. Sometimes it may be more appropriate to use answers for tutor guidance only unless the data set is pre-populated with data from "another" group to ensure that at least one "other" gave the same incorrect answer. However, the public presentation of results can also provide a valuable opportunity to help reduce feelings of isolation in cases where large numbers of students are expected to get the "wrong" answer. A successful activity used every year in the first teaching session involves students privately writing down the answers to a series of number calculations using "brain" and "calculator" with a request for volunteers willing to write their answers in the "brain" or "calculator" column on the board. The presence of a plastic "chocolate calculator" which does not use BODMAS rules (the mnemonic for the order of maths functions—Brackets, Orders, Division and Multiplication, Addition and Subtraction), the confusion with default settings of new calculators, inputting errors and student lack of familiarity with BODMAS generally ensure that a wide range of responses are generated in both columns and indeed encouraged, with a final class vote on the "correct" answer which normally turns out to be the incorrect one. Not only does this provide a successful introduction to the importance of operation order, but within a short time everyone in the group recognises that everyone else does not know everything.

The creation of learning partnerships between students who can scaffold (Wood et al., 1976) each other's learning is a valuable tool. However, very unequal partnerships can have the opposite effect, and it is sometimes helpful to remove those who are already proficient with a particular topic from the mix. If a topic is likely to be perceived as "very basic" by some members of the class (but not mastered or labelled in such a way by others), it is usually beneficial to provide a voluntary "opt out" option rather than attempt to have people working at different paces. It is difficult to begin teaching as far back as possible and to go at a pace near the slowest, when other members of the group are projecting their impatience. There is also a danger that this frustration results in an explicit labelling of this topic as easy or basic which does not build confidence for a student who is finding difficulty with that particular concept. It is also difficult for students to feel that they can ask questions. The notion that this opt out is voluntary implies a level of ownership of learning but also allows students to opt in without losing face.

Graduated Exposure: Reducing Test Anxiety and Panic

For some students maths tests and exams produce high levels of anxiety or panic. This anxiety may be less in evidence when using online multiple choice tests and similar resources administered through information technology (IT) blackboard systems and such tests remain valuable ways for students to check their own learning. However, since pen and paper tests remain an essential form of assessment, test anxiety needs to be reduced. Traditionally, tests are likely to bring together a number of different anxiety triggers which may impair function. The most obvious of these are the importance of the test for the future, the need to complete the test in silent isolation at a desk, the need to work to a time limit (see Walen and Williams (2002) for further discussion), the need to remember appropriate content, to use a range of skills and knowledge synoptically and to overcome panic which may have been developed through previous test experiences. Additionally, many tests are specifically designed to identify what people do not know rather than what they do, weaknesses rather than strengths (Gardner, 1999), not a process designed to raise levels of self-efficacy.

In something of a parallel with the graduated exposure process used for developing allergy resistance, a successful approach has been to introduce tests with as few triggers as possible and then gradually build them up. Small tests have been introduced from Week 2. For the very first test, the importance is limited because people can select to redo it, there is no time limit (within practical constraints), tests are open book and so notes and worked examples are available, the content is very narrow and predictable, based on questions similar to those previously met in worksheets and no synoptic skills are required. For those identifying very severe panic ahead of the first test, people are offered the opportunity to sit near the door and offered another attempt should they "bolt." Such an offer has usually been sufficient for a student to remain until the end. As the term progresses, the triggers are gradually reintroduced. Time limits far beyond those likely to be needed by any student are introduced and then slowly reduced. Opportunities to retake are removed but replaced by an awareness that each test is worth very few marks. One more challenging question, clearly labelled as such is added to begin to provide some discrimination in test marks. Although these tests remain "open book," the provision of a number of mock or practice exam and test papers start to prepare students to cope with assessments where notes will not be available. The essential part of this process is the provision of rapid and positive feedback. Successful completion of each test increases self-efficacy, increasing the likelihood of doing well in the next one. However, one final anxiety trigger needs to be remembered. Marked work *must* be handed back within a folder so that students can opt to look at their work surrounded by others or in privacy.

It is not possible to directly measure the change in anxiety levels caused by this exposure process for all students, but the individual success stories for those with extreme panic and their willingness to relate their story to others bears testimony to the efficacy of the process.

Avoiding Labels and Self- or Institutional Denigration

Those with low self-esteem and poor previous experience of maths sometimes give themselves labels and set their expectations accordingly:

> I'm probably totally wrong because like I said I'm rubbish at maths.
> (Student comment, Dodd, 2012, p. 120)

It is only through the raising of self-efficacy and achievement that these ideas can be changed. There are, however, occasions when institutions also label students sometimes through lack of awareness of potential damage. During a discussion about maths centre provision in some universities, it was mentioned that the word "support" had been removed from some publicity literature because it implied people were not doing as well as they should do. The word "remedial," sometimes associated with special learning needs and always implying that something is not quite as it should be and needs remedying or repairing, is totally inappropriate to be applied to any student but particularly to those who may have similar capabilities to others but perform less well because they have not yet been taught specific topics. Sadly, this term is frequently misused, undermining both the self-worth of students and the perceptions of value of the teaching undertaken.

The examples of practice described in this chapter have been selected to illustrate ways in which students, tutors and institutions can work together to overcome issues of negative emotions in maths and increase self-efficacy. Whilst each of the ideas described represents successful practice, by far the most important of all the ideas put forward in this chapter has to be the radical constructivist advice to consider learning through the eyes of the learner. It is, therefore, on this final reminder that the chapter concludes:

> When students genuinely engage in solving mathematical problems, they proceed in personally reasonable and productive ways.
> (Confrey, 1991, p. 111)

REFERENCES

Bandura, A. (1994). Self-efficacy. In Ramachandran V. S. (Ed.), *Encyclopaedia of human behaviour, vol. 4* (pp. 71–81). New York: Academic.

Benn, R. (1997). *Adults count too: Mathematics for empowerment*. Leicester: NIACE.

Bibby, T. (2002). Shame: An emotional response to doing mathematics as an adult and a teacher. *British Educational Research Journal, 28,* 705–721.

Buxton, L. (1981). *Do you panic about maths? Coping with maths anxiety*. London: Heinemann Educational Books.

Coben, D. (2000). Mathematics or common sense? Researching 'invisible' mathematics through adults' life histories. In D. Coben, J. O'Donoghue, & G. Fitzsimons (Eds.), *Perspectives on adults learning mathematics: Research and practice*. Dordrecht/Boston/London: Kluwer Academic Publishers.

Confrey, J. (1991). Learning to listen: A student's understanding of powers of ten. In E. von Glasersfeld (Ed.), *Radical constructivism in mathematics education*. Dordrecht/Boston/London: Kluwer Academic Publishers.

Dodd, M. (2012). *The influence of previous understanding and relative confidence on adult maths learning: Building adult understanding on a Brownfield site*. Doctorate in Education thesis: Open University.

Duffin, J., & Simpson, A. (2000). Understanding their thinking: The tension between the cognitive and the affective. In D. Coben, J. O'Donoghue, & G. FitzSimons (Eds.), *Perspectives on adults learning mathematics: Research and practice*. Dordrecht/Boston/London: Kluwer academic publishers.

Evans, J. (2000). *Adults' mathematical thinking and emotions: A study of numerate practice*. London/New York: Routledge Falmer.

Gardner, H. (1999). Assessment in context. In P. Murphy (Ed.), *Learners, learning and assessment*. London: Paul Chapman Publishing.

Karsenty, R. (2004). Mathematical self-schema: A framework for analyzing adults' retrospection on high school mathematics. *The Journal of Mathematical Behavior, 23,* 325–349.

Klinger, C. (2007). Experience, the difference: Maths attitudes and beliefs in commencing undergraduate students and pre-tertiary adult learners in the changing face of adults mathematics education: Learning from the past, planning for the future. *Proceedings of the 14th international conference of Adults Learning Maths—A research forum* (pp. 197–207). Ireland: University of Limerick.

Knowles, M. (1980). *The modern practice of adult education: From pedagogy to androgogy (2nd Edition)*. New York: Cambridge.

Lannin, J., Barker, D., & Townsend, B. (2007). How students view the general nature of their errors. *Educational Studies in Mathematics, 66,* 43–59.

Safford, K. (2000). Algebra for adult students: The student voices. In D. Coben, J. O'Donoghue, & G. FitzSimons (Eds.), *Perspectives on adults learning math-*

ematics: Research and practice. Dordrecht/Boston/London: Kluwer Academic Publishers.

Sewell, B. (1981). *Use of mathematics by adults in daily life.* Leicester: Advisory Council for Adult and Continuing Education.

Walen, S., & Williams, S. (2002). A matter of time: Emotional responses to timed mathematics tests. *Educational Studies in Mathematics, 49,* 361–378.

Wood, D., Bruner, S. J., & Ross, G. (1976). The role of tutoring in problem solving. *Journal of Child Psychology, 17,* 89–100.

CHAPTER 11

Students' Academic Emotions, Their Effects and Some Suggestions for Teaching Practices

Douglas P. Newton

The Emotional System

The emotional system tries to look after our best interests, or, at least, what it perceives to be in our best interests. It automatically and quickly appraises events and prompts us to action. If it judges an event to be in our interest, it responds with emotions like pleasure and prompts acceptance. If the event is seen as a threat to personal goals, values, or beliefs, it produces unpleasant feelings and prompts rejection. Our goals, values and beliefs may not be entirely conscious. For instance, as social animals, we usually want others to think well of us; we do not want them to see us as inept, insufferable, unreliable or stupid, but we do not (usually) bring that into consciousness and weigh an event against it—the emotional system does it all automatically. Of course, an event may seem innocuous to begin with, but on thinking about it (the intellectual system), threats to our goals and values may emerge and then our emotional system takes over (Lazarus, 1991). This appraisal theory, applied to classroom events, predicts emotions which can bear upon academic success, sometimes for

D.P. Newton (✉)
School of Education, University of Durham, Pelaw House,
Leazes Road, Durham DH1 1TA, UK

the better and sometimes for the worse. Typical classroom emotions can include anticipation, interest, satisfaction, pride and joy. They can, however, also include dread, anxiety, embarrassment and frustration. Pekrun and Linnenbrink-Garcia (2012) have called these, together, academic emotions, although they are not, of course, confined to the classroom. Academic emotions can affect students of all ages, but vary in likelihood and intensity according to age and context. For instance, mature students who are amongst young students may be particularly susceptible to some of the negative emotions. This, often automatic, process is summarised in Fig. 11.1.

STUDENTS AND THEIR EMOTIONAL RESPONSES

At least in part due to efforts to widen and extend participation in higher education (HE), the body of would-be students is more diverse than it once was. Amongst these are those who are older and with more varied entry qualifications than was once common. These commonly form a large proportion of students on access and foundation study courses. Their goals tend to centre on improving the quality of their employment prospects and on satisfying personal interests (Davies, Osborne, & Williams, 2002). This often entails considerable personal, social and financial risk, and so achieving these goals is a matter of some consequence. At the same time, they may perceive significant differences between themselves and students straight from school. Those who are older—some older than their tutors and old enough to be parents of their classmates—often believe that more is expected of their knowledge, abilities and performance, both by tutors and by other students. Those lacking some conventional entry qualifications

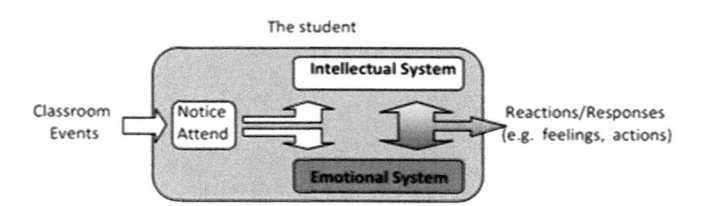

Fig. 11.1 A model of students' dual system for maintaining their well-being: events are noticed, judged for bearing upon goals, beliefs and values, and result in responses according to the judgements

(e.g. particular Advanced Level grades of the GCE in England) can also see themselves as less able, and socially and intellectually inferior to other students (Chapman, Parmar, & Trotter, 2008). To the extent that they value their self-esteem, self-image, public image, classroom activities and tutorials can be threatening and produce strong negative emotions (Perrin, O'neil, Grimes, & Bryson, 2014). For example, Newson, Mcdowell, and Saunders (2011) describes a 40-year-old student's feeling of exposure and her attempts to avoid looking "silly." Others felt humiliated and diminished. Even when such students work alone, online, they can feel fear and anxiety because they are unfamiliar with the technology or that way of studying. Some feel alienated, even lonely. Others, with home responsibilities, feel guilt at neglecting them (Zembylas, 2008). This guilt can extend to the almost inevitable changes they experience in themselves and which have the potential to affect relationships. For instance, they can be nervous about revealing their new perspectives to old friends and family, something which can attract their hostility and resentment (Brookfield, 1994). Providing feedback to such students can also threaten their sense of self and right to self-determination: Young (2000) describes some who found the process "annihilating," taking the feedback as a personal indictment. Of course, not all feel like that. Some, presumably those with strong self-esteem and a secure self-image, are less threatened by returning to the classroom and feel excited by it (Zembylas, 2008). But this illustrates that would-be HE students with such backgrounds can experience strong emotions, such as, embarrassment, humiliation, fear, anxiety, and guilt in academic contexts. Does it matter?

Emotions are not bad in themselves: they provide information intended to preserve or enhance well-being. In the classroom, they can promote and impede particular kinds of thinking. For instance, there is a lot of evidence that feeling blue can benefit analytical, logical, deductive thought. It tends to make thinkers focus on the detail—they look at the trees rather than the wood. On the other hand, feeling cheerful tells students that they are safe to throw caution to the winds, run the risk of being wrong, construct new meanings, speculate, and be creative. In other words, they can ignore the detail, the trees, and look at the bigger picture, the wood. Of course, life in the classroom is rarely so simple. At some point, creative ideas have to be evaluated, so emotions may need to be adjusted to give critical thinking a fair try (a more detailed and comprehensive account of these effects, including those of moods, is available in Newton, 2014). Many students have learned to adjust their state of mind to meet the needs of the task as it evolves, something often called emotional intelligence. Emotional intelligence is strongly associated with academic success (Parker, Summerfeldt, Hogan, & Majeski, 2004). Appropriate emotions oil the mind's cogs and facilitate success. But, some emotions can be like sand in the works and bring useful thought to a grinding halt.

When the Only Thing Between Students and Their Success Is Themselves

The grinding of cogs is most obvious for strong emotions, such as anger and elation, which take mental resources away from the task in hand (Pham, 2007). Such emotions must diminish before classroom thought can become purposeful and productive. Strong emotions of this kind are probably not the most common in the classroom. Anxiety, however, is one which is. A little anxiety can focus students' minds and help them perform better, but in the extreme, anxiety is well known for its disabling effects, particularly in course work and examinations which threaten personal goals (Connors, Putwain, Woods, & Nicholson, 2009). Some students drop out of school because of it and, without conventional qualifications, join those who might try to enter HE when older. If they do, they often have even more at stake than before—examination success really matters to them. Unfortunately, we sometimes add fear in order to motivate students to work harder for examinations when we remind them that poor results destroy life plans (Jackson, 2010). There are, however, other events which generate emotions that impede a student's success.

Public Performance: Everyone Looks at Me

Of particular relevance to the mature student and those with self-doubt is public performance. According to Terenzini, Pascarella, and Blimling (1999), students' personal interactions with others are the most powerful source of influence on their learning. At its simplest, this amounts to responding to tutors' questions. Asking questions is a common practice for stimulating purposeful thought and obtaining feedback on teaching effectiveness. Unfortunately, these students are likely to be particularly sensitive to threats to their self-esteem, self-image and public image. In short, they do not want to appear stupid. This seemingly innocuous tactic is perceived as a major threat and some students sit anxiously avoiding the tutor's eye and hoping to be ignored. The effect is to reduce their participation (Weaver & Qi, 2005; Stoeckli, 2010) or, at least, make them very cautious about it. Perhaps more threatening are those events which call upon such students to present a public review of some body of work. In Western cultures, there is a strong tendency to be negative and to engage in fault-finding and point-scoring (Newton, 2010). The dread of this response makes it difficult for the student to do herself justice—and not all students are from the West—which introduces another aspect of public performance. Having to respond in a second language can generate embarrassment and tongue-tying emotions, very like stage fright (Horwitz, 2010). We sometimes forget that academic language, subject vocabulary and precise expression can, in effect, be like another language for some students (Rees, Bruce, & Bradley, 2014). They, too, can be subject to public performance emotions until (and if) their academic language skills become fairly automatic. Already mentioned is the provision of feedback on the students' work. As it directly threatens goals and aspirations, it is clearly threatening and is a source of strong emotions. Moreover, an older student receiving critical feedback from a much younger tutor can find it difficult (Newton, 2014).

It is important to emphasise that not all students respond adversely to such events. People are different and some have acquired ways of dealing with the threats. For instance, some older students attempt to lower expectations by prefacing their interaction with phrases like, "It may be a stupid question, but…," "I must be very slow today because I didn't quite grasp…," and, "It's a long time since I did this kind of thing but…." In this way, they avoid a loss of face but possibly at the expense of self-esteem and self-image.

Some Thoughts About Teaching Practices

Clearly, as far as academic success is concerned, the intellect is not everything. Students can have a strong intellect and still fail. Emotions are not always the cause; ill health, lack of funds, family commitments and the absence of opportunity are others which enter into it, but emotions do come between some students and success. We may, however, be able to alleviate the problem with some forethought.

Pre-course Preparation of Students

Many students will arrive feeling more or less apprehensive. It would help if pre-course case studies were provided to illustrate the normality of particular worries, the extent to which many are ill-founded, and to offer some strategies for coping with them. Coupland (2003) recommends that opportunities are provided for informal conversations amongst students early in their courses. A pre-course electronic portal with short talks about their courses, including video clips introducing tutors, and enabling students to share their hopes and concerns with others, can certainly help to allay fears. For example, one mature student's mixed feelings were evident when she wrote, "I'm just one big bundle of excitement and apprehension at the minute... The website is great...." Another thought the website was "a godsend" which "made you feel part of something." A third, still overseas, said she was nervous but tutors and students reassured her. One student concluding with "We are a very friendly bunch" (Nolan, 2014).

Preparing Teaching Materials

When planning teaching, a lot of thought goes into exercising the students' intellect. But, the intellect is not everything, and there needs to be forethought about fostering a productive partnership between the intellect and the emotions. This means, at the least, avoiding conflict between the two systems. It should begin with the design of teaching and learning materials, and environments. Plass, Heidig, Hayward, Homer, and Um (2013, pp. 2–3) were particularly interested in designing multimedia materials ("involving pictures, animations, narration, videos and text in computer-based environments") to foster positive emotions, something they called "emotional design." While strategies for inducing particular emotions at or before the beginning of a learning session may have some useful effect, they argue that building it into the design of the materials is likely to sustain the effect as the task progresses. For instance, saturated and warm colours (such as yellow and orange) have been found to "increase pleasure." Anthropomorphic figures in illustrations have a similar effect. Um, Plass, Hayward, and Homer (2011), testing colour and figure in combination on graduate students studying education in Germany, found that they also reduced perceptions of task difficulty and increased self-reported motivation. Here, some attributes of the study need to be held in mind. The average age of the students tested was 22 years, most were female and graduates. Will, for instance, older students find cartoon-like figures patronising? Tutors will need to be sensitive to such possibilities and adjust their emotional design to allow for them. Multimedia also draws on other means of communication, such as sound.

The extent to which this affects emotions is not clear. Nevertheless, such studies offer food for thought and room for classroom experimentation. The next step is to consider the emotional climate in the classroom.

In the Classroom

The emotional climate is the general, prevailing emotional tone of a group at a given time. Tutors will have noticed how two groups can respond differently to identical sessions. There are several reasons for this, but the emotional climate is a significant one. Moreover, some students can dominate the situation and their moods are transmitted to others. The climate, however, is not fixed. Tutors need to be aware that they are leading players on their own stage and their states of mind can be contagious, too. For instance, when students have to be creative, continual reminders of the shortage of time can induce self-defeating anxiety and frustration. Equally, a tutor's overly light-hearted approach to critical thinking can set the tone for a state of mind which is not best suited to this kind of purposeful thought. Public performances in particular need careful planning and handling. To begin with, these might be small-scale performances given to sub-groups of like students (Newton, 2014). After small-scale exposure, many students will be able to progress to full group presentations. Expectations of performer and audience need to be clear and considerate and strategies planned for occasions when "stage fright" gets the better of the performer. This is what should be a part of routine planning for what is, in effect, emotional labour, something which would probably help all students, whatever their background. Concern here is for those who are particularly susceptible to threats to their personal goals and values which make their learning a miserable and challenging experience and, in the process, limit their achievement. These may need further attention after the class.

After the Class

Interaction does not, of course, end in the classroom. Generally, work is set and graded, feedback is provided, examinations are set and marked, and tutorials are given on the outcomes. Unfortunately, these are often direct threats to older students' goals, bringing the high level of risk to the surface, and generating a lot of anxiety. This anxiety, in excess, can adversely affect performance. The subsequent feedback, intended to support improvement, threatens fragile egos and is taken personally. The response can be fight or flight. Again, the tutor should prepare for this. Bland feedback has little remedial or instructive value, so inevitably, it must point to ways of improving the student's work. One approach would be to ask the student to comment on the strengths and weaknesses of the assignment as though it had been written by the tutor. Then, keeping distance between the feedback and the student, the tutor reflects aloud on the work: "If this was my essay, I would be pleased with…; I would have added a piece there about…; I think I would have said that this view is doubtful because…." The student is brought back in at this point for his views about the reflections and is asked to sum up how such assignments may be improved in general. In this way, the student is involved in the evaluation and the feeling of being judged by others is reduced. (Not all students need such an approach. Some are able to suspend their adulthood on the doorstep and regress to an acceptance of school-style judgement (Hanson, 1998).) This is not, of course, the end of it. Students often have to do tests and examinations.

Tests and Examinations

Pekrun, Elliot, and Maier (2009) see students' test anxiety as a series of emotion-inducing events extending over time (Fig. 11.2). As the test approaches, a time when we might expect students to prepare for the test, anxiety increases. This can affect the quality of their preparation. If anxiety persists and is severe during the test, it can impede recall and purposeful thought. For high-stake tests, anxiety generally increases as the date of the results approaches. Emotions follow—positive or negative—and then usually slowly fade with time. For students who take the risk and give a year of their lives to a chance to enter HE, tests can be a major source of worry. Clearly, only emotions felt before and during the test can affect the outcome, so interventions here can make a difference to attainment. Self-efficacy is the belief in one's capacity to organise and execute the courses of action needed to handle difficult situations (Bandura, 1997). As self-efficacy increases, test anxiety decreases (Onyeizugbo, 2010). Making students aware of the benefits of taking control with a plan, of having goals and priorities, and of having a timetable and consciously using mastery strategies is a start (Cismas, 2009). Study skills help here: mind maps, for instance, can provide succinct aids to memory and can also be used to construct responses to examination questions. Emotions

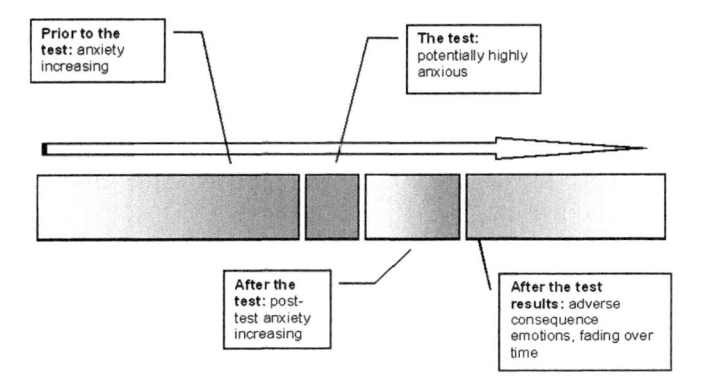

```
┌─────────────────┐              ┌─────────────────┐
│ Prior to the    │              │ The test:       │
│ test: anxiety   │              │ potentially     │
│ increasing      │              │ highly anxious  │
└─────────────────┘              └─────────────────┘
         │         ╲              ╱         │
         │          ╲            ╱          │
═════════▼═══════════▼══════════▼═══════════▼═════════▶
                              ╱        ╲
                             ╱          ╲
                 ┌─────────────┐         ┌──────────────────┐
                 │ After the   │         │ After the test   │
                 │ test: post- │         │ results: adverse │
                 │ test anxiety│         │ consequence      │
                 │ increasing  │         │ emotions, fading │
                 └─────────────┘         │ over time        │
                                         └──────────────────┘
```

Fig. 11.2 The development of anxieties before, during and after a high-stake test

generated by the test itself can be reduced by clarifying expectations (e.g. "These are examples of good responses to typical examination questions. They are 'good' because..."), and the form and mechanics of the test (Stipeck, 2002). Continuous assessment tends to make students less anxious than all-or-nothing, one-off examinations. Giving students frequent tests can also help to desensitise them to their threat, but note that some sophisticated, computer-run tests, such as those which quickly adapt to the students' upper cognitive limits, give little time for students to calm themselves before they meet difficult questions and can make those with a tendency to be anxious more so (Ortner & Caspers, 2011).

Building Resilience

Considerate teaching may help students make the most of their abilities, but sooner or later, he will meet tutors who are inconsiderate, insensitive or simply do not care. Does acknowledging the role of emotions in learning do any favours for these students? If it is done furtively, they are unlikely to learn much from it. Meeting less accommodating tutors later could be at least disturbing and even alarming with the risk of precipitating dropout. The long-term value of ensuring that emotions are the oil and not the sand in the works lies in students learning to brush sand out and add oil themselves. To develop some capacity for this kind of resilience, the actions taken should not be something done to students but something done with them. Bringing students inside the process of making the interaction of emotions and cognition productive gives them a chance to learn from it. Including it in study skills courses could also develop the capacity for self-regulation which would support further academic study (e.g. Benor, Ledger, Toussaint, Hett, & Zaccaro, 2009; Bradley et al., 2010; Kaviani, Javaheri, & Hatami, 2011). To that end, some simple strategies have been found useful:

- Music: As Shakespeare knew, music really does calm the troubled breast (quiet background music can also improve test scores after a lecture (see Dosseville, Laborde, & Scelles, 2012)).
- Exercise: A 30-minute spell of exercise, in particular, has been found to be very effective in reducing anxiety. It may be that the state of readiness for action induced by an anxious state is co-opted by the activity. The exercise can also increase the quality of the attention given to the task which follows it (Kubesch et al., 2009; Hogan et al., 2013; Stroth et al., 2009). But note that exercise can increase aggression (White & Kight, 1984), and those who have just exercised can be more emotionally affected by feedback (Turnbull & Wolfson, 2002).
- Social interaction: Talking with friends can make a difference, but they have to be the right ones. Saturnine friends can make moods worse.
- Relaxation: Progressively relaxing the body and clearing the mind using methods such as those used in mindfulness and meditation activity are known to be effective but know-how and practice are needed (Chen et al., 2012).

Thayer, Newman, & McClain (1994) recommend that, for the best results, a combination of strategies is used. They also remind us that there can be gender differences in preferences for strategies. For instance, men tend to prefer distraction, while women tend to prefer social interaction. It may also be necessary to remind students that these should not become substitutes for academic activity or a justification for or part of prevarication. The interaction between emotions and the intellect is also two-way, and these strategies can be strengthened by an intellectual reinterpretation of the threat. For instance, some events may present threats to the status quo and, at first, generate anxiety, but on reflection, some can offer palatable, even welcome, opportunities and then they produce anticipation. Clouds can have silver linings.

Conclusion

Popularly, being at least moderately happy is seen as the "correct" or optimum state (at least in the West). There may be a temptation to try to change all negative moods and emotions into positive ones, but temporary dysphoria is a part of life, and it has been argued that it has evolved because it serves a useful function in signalling that there is something about a person's well-being which needs attention (Forgas, 2013). As Frijda (1986) has put it, the mind has not evolved for happiness but for survival, and emotions, positive or negative, are there to support that end. However, moods and emotions can support or hinder activities not directly related to survival, like those in the classroom. Managing them has advantages, and it must be said, some students can do that by deploying their "emotional intelligence" (Parker et al., 2004). Others cannot do that or find themselves in situations which challenge their emotional intelligence. There are also students with deep emotional disturbances who may need specialist support. But for most students, Larsen (2000, p. 140), referring to moods, sums it up well: "I am not of the view that affective states should be regulated out of existence or that people should not have moods. We want people to have moods, but we don't necessarily want moods to have people."[1] And we should remember, some emotions are a source of motivation and support for productive, purposeful thought.

Although the context here is access to and foundation courses for HE, at a time of widening participation, the proportion of mature students with alternative educational backgrounds in the undergraduate body is likely to increase. The need to plan for both the intellectual and the emotional systems when teaching may, perhaps, increasingly extend across that student body.

Note

1. Moods are commonly distinguished from emotions. Emotions are generated by specific events and are often of fairly limited duration; moods are more diffuse, enduring, and reflect responses to perceptions of ongoing well-being. This chapter has focused on emotions, but moods also interact with cognition similarly. For example, negative moods, like depression, cause rumination, which takes mental resources away from the task in hand. Longer lasting are dispositions which can be seen as traits. For details, see Newton (2014).

References

Bandura, A. (1997). *Self-efficacy: The exercise of control*. New York: Freeman.
Benor, D. J., Ledger, K., Toussaint, L., Hett, G., & Zaccaro, D. (2009). Pilot study of emotional freedom techniques. *Explore, 5*(6), 338–340.
Bradley, R. T., Mccraty, R., Atkinson, M., Tomasino, D., Daugherty, A., & Arguelles, L. (2010). Emotion self-regulation, psychophysiological coherence, and test anxiety. *Applied Psychophysiology and Biofeedback, 35*(4), 261–283.
Brookfield, S. (1994). Tales from the dark side. *International Journal of Lifelong Education, 13*(3), 203–216.
Chapman, A., Parmar, D., & Trotter, E. (2008). An evaluation of the first year experience from the mature students' perspective. *Practitioner Research in Higher Education, 1*(1), 15–19.
Chen, K. W., Berger, C. C., Mannheimer, E., Forde, D., Magisdon, J., & Dachman, L. (2012). Meditative therapies for reducing anxiety. *Depression & Anxiety, 29*(7), 545–562.
Cismas, S. C. (2009). Test anxiety and motivational incentives in web-based learning. In I. Rudas, M. Demivalp, & N. Mastorakis (Eds.), *Proceedings of the 9th WSEAS conference on distance learning and web engineering* (pp. 77–82). Stevens Point: WSEAS.
Connors, L., Putwain, D., Woods, K., & Nicholson, L. (2009). Causes and consequences of test anxiety in Key Stage 2 pupils. *Paper presented at the BERA Conference*, September, Manchester.
Coupland, J. (2003). Small talk: Social functions. *Research on Language and Social Interactions, 36*, 1–6.
Davies, P., Osborne, M., & Williams, J. (2002). *For me or not for me? That is the question: Research report 297*. Norwich: HMSO.
Dosseville, F., Laborde, S., & Scelles, N. (2012). Music during lectures. *Learning and Individual Differences, 22*, 258–262.
Forgas, J. P. (2013). Don't worry, be sad! On the cognitive, motivational and interpersonal benefits of negative mood. *Current Directions in Psychological Science, 22*(3), 225–232.
Frijda, N. H. (1986). *The emotions*. Cambridge: Cambridge University Press.
Hanson, A. (1998). The search for a separate theory of adult learning. In R. Edwards, A. Hanson, & P. Raggatt (Eds.), *Boundaries of adult learning*. London: Routledge.
Hogan, M., Kiefer, M., Kubesch, S., Collins, P., Kilmartin, L., & Brosnan, M. (2013). The interactive effects of physical fitness and acute aerobic exercise on electrophysiological coherence and cognitive performance in adolescents. *Experimental Brain Research, 229*, 85–96.
Horwitz, E. K. (2010). Foreign and second language anxiety. *Language Teaching, 43*, 154–167.

Jackson, C. (2010). Fear in education. *Educational Review, 62*(1), 39–52.
Kaviani, H., Javaheri, F., & Hatami, N. (2011). Mindfulness-based cognitive therapy reduces depression and anxiety induced by real stressful setting in non-clinical population. *International Journal of Psychology and Psychological Therapy, 11*(2), 285–296.
Kubesch, S., Walk, L., Spitzer, M., Kammer, T., Lainburg, A., & Heim, R. (2009). A 30-minute physical education program improves students' executive attention. *Mind, Brain, and Education, 3*, 235–242.
Larsen, R. J. (2000). Toward a science of mood regulation. *Psychological Inquiry, 11*(3), 129–141.
Lazarus, R. S. (1991). *Emotion and adaptation*. New York: Oxford University Press.
Newson, C., Mcdowell, A., & Saunders, M. (2011). *Understanding the support needs of mature students*. Guilford: University Of Surrey.
Newton, D. P. (2010). Quality and peer review of research: An adjudicating role for editors. *Accountability in Research, 17*, 130–145.
Newton, D. P. (2014). *Thinking with feeling*. London: Routledge.
Nolan, S. (2014). Personal communication, 9 July 2014.
Onyeizugbo, E. U. (2010). Self-efficacy, gender and trait anxiety as moderators of text anxiety. *Electronic Journal of Research in Educational Psychology, 8*(1), 299–312.
Ortner, T. M., & Caspers, J. (2011). Consequences of test anxiety on adaptive testing versus fixed item testing. *European Journal of Psychological Assessment, 27*(3), 157–163.
Parker, J. D. A., Summerfeldt, L. J., Hogan, M. J., & Majeski, S. A. (2004). Emotional intelligence and academic success. *Personality and Individual Differences, 36*, 163–172.
Pekrun, R., Elliot, A. J., & Maier, M. A. (2009). Achievement goals and achievement emotions. *Journal of Educational Psychology, 101*(1), 115–135.
Pekrun, R., & Linnenbrink-Garcia, L. (2012). Academic emotions and student engagement. In S. L. Christenson, A. L. Reschly, & C. Wylie (Eds.), *Handbook of research on student engagement* (pp. 259–282). New York: Springer.
Perrin, J., O'neil, J., Grimes, A., & Bryson, L. (2014). Do learners fear more than fear itself. *Journal of Education and Training Studies, 2*(2), 67–75.
Pham, M. T. (2007). Emotions and rationality. *Review of General Psychology, 11*(2), 155–178.
Plass, J. L., Heidig, S., Hayward, E. O., Homer, B. D., & Um, E. (2013). Emotional design in multimedia learning. *Learning & Instruction*. Available from: doi:10.1016/j.learninstruct.2013.02.006
Rees, S., Bruce, M., & Bradley, S. (2014). Utilising data-driven learning in chemistry teaching: A shortcut to improving chemical language comprehension. *New Directions, 10*(1). Available from: doi:10.11120/Ndir.2014.00028

Stipeck, D. (2002). *Motivation to learn*. Boston: Allyn & Bacon.

Stoeckli, G. (2010). The role of individual and social factors in classroom loneliness. *The Journal of Educational Research, 103*, 28–39.

Stroth, S., Kubesch, S., Dieterie, K., Ruchsow, M., Heim, R., & Kiefer, M. (2009). Physical fitness, but not acute exercise modulates event-related potential indices for executive control in healthy adolescents. *Brain Research, 1269*, 114–124.

Terenzini, P. T., Pascarella, E. T., & Blimling, G. S. (1999). Students' out of class experiences and their influence on learning and cognitive development. *Journal of College Student Development, 40*, 610–623.

Thayer, R. E., Newman, J. R., & McClain, T. M. (1994). Self-regulation of mood. *Journal of Personality and Social Psychology, 67*(5), 910–925.

Turnbull, M., & Wolfson, S. (2002). Effects of exercise and outcome feedback on mood. *Journal of Sport Behaviour, 25*, 394–406.

Um, E., Plass, J. L., Hayward, E. O., & Homer, B. D. (2011). Emotional design in multimedia learning. *Journal of Educational Psychology*. Available from: doi:10.1037/A0026609

Weaver, R. R., & Qi, J. (2005). Classroom organization and participation. *The Journal of Higher Education, 76*(5), 570–601.

White, G. L., & Kight, T. D. (1984). Misattribution of arousal and attraction. *Journal of Experimental Social Psychology, 20*, 55–64.

Young, P. (2000). 'I might as well give up': Self-esteem and mature students' feelings about feedback on assignments. *Journal of Further and Higher Education, 24*(3), 409–418.

Zembylas, M. (2008). Adult learners' emotions in online learning. *Distance Education, 29*(1), 71–87.

CHAPTER 12

Stories with a Foundation

Catherine A. Marshall

INTRODUCTION

In this book, the contributors have outlined some of the reasons why some groups of people may be under-represented in higher education (HE). These are, of course, complex but are likely to include inadequate compulsory education, bias in the recruitment processes, and the alienation some people feel when they meet the dominant culture in HE. In addition, we have described some ways of overcoming obstacles and addressing the needs of non-traditional students through foundation programmes. We anticipate that readers will be able to relate these to their own situations and, if necessary, adapt or develop them to meet particular needs. We have been able to follow the subsequent progress of a number of students as they continued their studies as undergraduates. In this final chapter, we give these students a voice by drawing on interviews with three of them—whom we have called Rachel, Matt and Dan—to illustrate what they found to be important about their foundation year. We begin with some background context for each of them.

C.A. Marshall (✉)
Foundation Centre, University of Durham, Pelaw House, Leazes Road, Durham
DH1 1TA, UK

© The Editor(s) (if applicable) and The Author(s) 2016
C.A. Marshall et al. (eds.), *Widening Participation, Higher Education and Non-Traditional Students*,
DOI 10.1057/978-1-349-94969-4_12

Rachel

Rachel was one of the first students to join the foundation year in 1997. She was 21 years old and had left a local school when she was 16 to join Project 2000, a programme for the recruitment of nurses. Her sister's newly diagnosed illness gave her a fear of needles and blood and she withdrew from the nursing course. She then went to a further education (FE) college, still interested in health programmes, and took some vocational courses and an AS level in Spanish. None of the qualifications enabled her to access university degree courses, and Rachel was advised to take an Access course. On the completion of the courses, she was still not able to access a degree directly, so she started the foundation year programme instead.

The foundation programme was her route to a degree in Human Sciences, an anthropology degree with a strong focus on health. She achieved a 2:1 and then secured various jobs in health and social care. After gaining a position as a Health Promotion Specialist for Sure Start, she took a further, Open University, degree in Health Promotion and was chosen to take a funded master's degree in Public Health. As part of her master's degree, she commissioned an education pack for children which has become a successful commercial venture. From there, she took a Postgraduate Certificate in Education (PGCE), and is currently teaching Health and Social Care while putting together a literature review in order to apply for funding for a PhD in a subject related to health education.

Matt

Matt left a comprehensive school with, as he puts it, "nothing but a swimming certificate." He joined the army before even taking any end of school examinations and spent several years as a soldier. On his return to civilian life, he found himself contemplating a career either as a long distance lorry driver or as a security guard. When supporting his mother during her final illness, however, he found the motivation to try for a medical qualification. After taking an Access course, which was not sufficient to further his aspirations, he joined the foundation programme and, at the end of the year, went on to study a medical degree. Once qualified, he worked for a while as a surgeon, and then became a general practitioner.

Dan

Dan left school at 16, having been told that he was not academic enough to benefit from further study. He had a number of occupations, including making body jewellery and working in a nightclub and a public house. By his late 20s, his general reading had somehow given him an interest in philosophy and he decided to follow a foundation programme so he could take his interest further. He did so with admirable success, achieving a first-class degree in Philosophy, followed by a master's degree with distinction, and is now studying for a PhD.

Overcoming Inadequate Initial Education

As outlined in the first chapter, Bourdieu's (1973) view was that schools tended to favour middle-class children, rewarding social and cultural capital rather than ability. All three of the interviewees described poor or inadequate school experiences:

> So school was shit from start to finish, I hated school, liked design and technology, but the rest was pure dross.
> (Matt)

> School for me wasn't the best place so my grades at school weren't what I was projected to get.
> (Rachel)

> I imagine prison is quite similar to my school.
> (Dan)

Both Rachel and Matt had reasons for their problems at school. Rachel felt she had a range of problems, while Matt had undiagnosed dyslexia:

> … although in all honesty I hold my hands up and go, "Well, it's this person to blame," because it wasn't, it was a multitude of things, mixing with the wrong crowd, my parents splitting up, it could have been all of those things together.
> (Rachel)

> I couldn't really read, and I could make out what words: I knew what words were but I couldn't make up a sentence and they just didn't make sense and I got headaches doing it, so I just thought, "Nope," I'd look at the pictures, I'd ask someone else.
> (Matt)

All three believed that more could have been done for them:

> ... but I feel very much sitting here truthfully and honestly that because I was seen as that type of person that wasn't going to really going to do much with their life, there was no support or anything given to me to try to be better, I was just one of them that well you're not concentrating and you don't do this and you don't do that, we are not going to give you the time that is required for you to go any further.
> (Rachel)

> I think 'cos of my size they just figured "lump" so as long as I was quiet, because I wasn't disruptive, I think I just sailed under the radar.
> (Matt)

> I didn't care about the schoolwork, it just didn't interest me, it wasn't fun, you know there was the odd bit which was fun, and it makes you think they could do a lot more in schools to recognise the difference between somebody being stupid and somebody being bored and not interested.
> (Dan)

At various points both Dan and Matt were actively discouraged from following their aspirations. For Dan, that was at school when he inquired about taking A levels at a sixth-form college:

> ... the school careers advisor, yea, she was just like, "no your marks are too low, you can't do A levels" ... she said, "you're not academically inclined," or something like that!
> (Dan)

For Matt it happened when he was taking his Access course and he had completed his university application form, aiming for a course in medicine. He remembers the date of his conversation with his advisor:

> 16 October 2001 ... my tutor sat me down, we were doing how to fill in my UCAS form and she ... said, "Do you think you should put some other options in." I said, "No, I just want that [Medicine] on." She said, "You're not going to get into Medicine." I said, "Really?" "No." I said, "Why not?" She said, "You're not 18, you haven't got 5 O levels at grade A; you're just not." I said, "Well, we will try though, shan't we, then we'll know." And she went, "Well, the closing date for that was yesterday so we will have to wait till next year." I said, "It's no good telling me that now when I could have had it in, it's all done." She said, "We thought you weren't going to get in,

so there was no point. We thought we'd just put something else, and you would get onto a[nother] degree."
(Matt)

Matt and Rachel had both taken Access courses but then moved on to a foundation programme, because they found that the Access course did not provide the route into the degrees that they wanted. In Matt's case, he described being quite reluctant to retake what was an equivalent year, but then realised the value of the course. Rachel also describes what she sees as the value of the foundation year:

> At first I was, like, at first I was a little bit like, I've done all of this, but it's a completely different ball game, the stuff taught was a world apart from what I had done previously; one guy came from my course to do biomed at the same place, lasted about a month, they just hadn't prepared us for degree-level work at all and I think that became apparent quite quickly.
> (Matt)

> I think that if I hadn't done the foundation, if I had only done the Access, which is what a lot of people do nowadays, I don't think it gives them that grounding ... Because of my role now, I work at the college where I deliver on the foundation and I deliver on the BTEC—I think that foundation for me gave me that progression route that I needed.
> (Rachel)

Chapters 3, 4 and 5 address some of the issues with inadequate initial education, which may include missing out on specific gaps in knowledge, for example, how to use laboratory equipment, incomplete levels of education and missing out on the implicit curriculum. Matt describes being actively excluded from his English classes at school:

> At school, they recognised I couldn't write, I couldn't form letters, so they gave me this typewriter with a little LCD screen on it and a roll of heat dot matrix paper, but whenever you pressed return it made this noise and the thing went across and back and the teacher just said I'm not having you in class with noise, go and sit in the corridor with it, so that was English fourth and fifth year; so it was good crack! We didn't have phones then so I used to sit and doodle for three hours a week.
> (Matt)

All three interviewees found their subject content useful in their progression routes:

> I do remember doing quite a lot of the foundation modules and finding them really interesting. They actually were a really good stepping stone for my degree because it gave me the genetics parts, gave me an awfully good knowledge background to enable me to progress easily onto the health and human sciences, because I didn't have A level science. Although I had got my dual science at school GCSE, it certainly was a lot different, so that foundation element gave me that really good knowledge to progress to that level.
> (Rachel)

> The kids that had done A levels, even the ones that had done philosophy A level were less well prepared than we were, in terms of searching for things like academic journals, referencing and writing bibliographies, and things like that. Other first years knew nothing about that stuff. The A level, it's a textbook, and you regurgitate it in an exam, also we were getting good marks straight away ... I think with the A level route takes people from what I have observed, it takes a lot longer to start getting good at the university level because it is so different, you know, because you learn by what you have written, what you have read in a textbook, and you spew it all out in an exam and you'll get 90 % in an exam, you do that in a university essay you'll get a 2.2 probably.
> (Dan)

> That's what the foundation programme tells you ... you need to find your own way of studying; not everything works for everyone.
> (Matt)

OVERCOMING RECRUITMENT BIAS

Chapter 6 explored the difficulties of selecting non-traditional students, and the importance of achieving social mobility through access to HE. Moreton's categories of description help think about applicants who may benefit from studying for a foundation year. These have been broadly split into "Driving Force" and "Assets," and elements of driving force were evident in all the three interviewees. Dan described developing his interest in philosophy by reading widely, Rachel described her many and varied approaches to following her interest in health prior to finding a foundation programme, and Matt talked about his desire to improve himself:

I love learning, and I don't think I ever will stop from doing my postgraduate Health and Social Care. After I have done my master's, PGCE hopefully, I'll do my PhD, and then I'll maybe look at something else. I just enjoy reading ... I enjoy researching. I wish that all of this was picked up a lot earlier on and that somebody had homed in on the fact that I actually did want to learn, and I wasn't one of those children that just didn't care.
(Rachel)

Yes—my old job was crap and getting pulled away and it was just no life for her [my daughter] and then I was frustrated as a person not doing something that I enjoyed and wanted to do, my options as I saw them, what everyone was doing was HGV [heavy goods vehicles] or security ... so I was looking for something and then once I had started reading, the world kind of opened up really.
(Matt)

I wanted to do philosophy; I had always been interested in it. Since leaving school I had become interested in various things; I did a lot of reading on whatever topics, and I became interested in philosophy during my, I guess during my late to mid-20s.
(Dan)

There also seems to be an important element of self-belief and habits of mind, including persistence and determination. Rachel, for example, tried vocational qualifications such as Project 2000 and General National Vocational Qualifications (GNVQs), as well as an AS level and an Access course, before starting a foundation year. There also seems to be a determination to succeed, despite the barriers. Dan said that:

... because that determination is pretty important; pushing against expectations, I think.
(Dan)

Overcoming Alienation with the Dominant Culture in HE

The later chapters in the book describe the importance of belonging and being an accepted part of the group to help build the emotional security for learning to take place. Dan describes his and his father's thoughts on his application and acceptance for a foundation year:

I thought [it] was this kind of posh university. I didn't think I would have much of a chance at getting in and I remember my Dad saying when I got in, "Gosh, I can't believe you've got in, I was thinking that's ridiculous applying [there]."
(Dan)

And being a mature student highlighted differences:

… definitely it's a very strange place to be a mature student …
(Dan)

The thing is, being mature, time seems more valuable than it actually is, so that year was really a bit uphill at the start.
(Matt)

Dan also felt out of place at times for a different reason:

I mean the other undergraduates, you know, they were pleasant, I made friends with some, but I never really felt like I was one of them.
(Dan)

Dan went so far as to describe his experiences as "imposter syndrome":

But yeah, it's weird. I still have a massive imposter syndrome, I just feel like I'm not supposed [to be here]. I always feel like everybody is doing more work than me, or everybody is more sort of, I don't know, it's hard to explain, but there's always the feeling that I've done as best as I've done. When I did the foundation year, I was worrying that I wasn't good enough to do a degree; when I did the degree, that I'm not good enough to do a master's, and now I've got my master's, I'm not good enough to do my PhD, so, yes, there is always a sense of not belonging.
(Dan)

This feeling was echoed by Matt:

I've been waiting for that day for someone to tap me on the shoulder and say you're in the wrong place, move!
(Matt)

Imposter syndrome, first described in connection with women in business in the 1970s (Clance & Imes, 1978), has been widely investigated in academia. Subsequent research has found that more than 70 % of people experience aspects of imposter syndrome at some stage (Gravois, 2007).

It has been argued that for non-traditional, mature students these feelings of not belonging are severe enough to require remedy (Chapman, 2015), and that for first-generation students, this can be a real barrier (Gardner & Holley, 2011). This feeling may not be altogether without basis. Sadly, Dan recalls a conversation with a senior academic who felt that there should be no need to widen participation in HE.

Feed Forward

Despite, or perhaps because of, the lack of aspiration-raising that the three participants experienced when growing up, they do express a desire to support and help others. Rachel is doing this quite actively in her teaching at a local FE college:

> Why I want to be a teacher now, is that I want to help the people who are less fortunate than me now in my situation, that are just not getting the time that they require or deserve.
> (Rachel)

Matt is interested in providing bursaries for other foundation students because he recognises the impact of education on his life:

> ... just it's unbelievable, the trajectory, that's the thing, it alters the trajectory of where your life, where your kid's life is going to go after that, it's mind blowing, it really is.
> (Matt)

While the widening of participation in HE is often seen as meeting the needs of society and of the economy, these glances into ex-foundation year students' lives also serves to remind us of the impact widening participation can have on individuals.

References

Bourdieu, P. (1973). Cultural reproduction and social reproduction. In R. Brown (Ed.), *Knowledge, education, and cultural change*. London: Tavistock.

Chapman, A. (2015). Using the assessment process to overcome imposter syndrome in mature students. *Journal of Further and Higher Education*. doi:10.1080/0309877X.2015.1062851.

Clance, P. R., & Imes, S. (1978). The imposter phenomenon in high achieving women: Dynamics and therapeutic intervention. *Psychotherapy Theory, Research and Practice, 15*(3), 241–247.

Gardner, S. K., & Holley, K. A. (2011). "Those invisible barriers are real": The progression of first-generation students through doctoral education. *Equity and Excellence in Education, 44*(1), 77–92.

Gravois, J. (2007). You're not fooling anyone. *The Chronicle of Higher Education*, 9th November 2007. Retrieved from http://chronicle.com/article/You-re-Not-Fooling-Anyone/28069

INDEX

A
academic discipline, 30
academic emotions, 166
academic vocabulary, 43, 44
Academic Word List (AWL), 44
Access course, 24, 26, 27, 29, 31, 180, 183, 185
acculturation, 134, 143–5
adaptive media, 84–5
additional language support, 42–3
admissions process, 91–5
affective processes, 59
Alatorre, S., 63
Albrechtslund, A., 107–8
A-level system, 5–8, 92
Al-Shuailib, A., 76
ambivalence, 96, 97
Andrade, M. S., 123
anxiety, 60, 74, 78, 152–4, 159–61
Art and Design courses, 32
audio feedback, 51–2

Aufschnaiter, S. V., 76
Augmented Reality (AR), 78

B
Bacon, R., 76
Bakx, A., 96
Bandura, A., 155, 156
Barker, D., 155
Barnes, N. G., 106
Bergen, T., 96
Berger, P., 10, 137, 144
Bernhard, J., 79
Bibby, T., 151, 157
Big Five, 95
Biggs, 84
Black and Minority Ethnic students, 11–, 25
Blanden, J., 21
Blimling, G. S., 168
Bodycott, P., 141

Note: Page number followed by 'n' refers to endnotes.

Boliver, V., 8, 9, 22
Bourdieu, P., 1–3, 5–7, 9, 10, 13, 137, 181
Bowl, M., 9, 146
Brackets, Orders, Division and Multiplication, Addition and Subtraction (BODMAS) rules, 159
Brinko, K. T., 52
Brownfield site, 59, 61
Buxton, L., 151, 154, 157
Byram, M., 144

C
capital, 1–2. *See also* cultural capital
Carstensen, A.-K., 79
Cassels, J., 45
Cayless, A., 76
Cela-Ranilla, J. M., 96
Chemistry, 76–7, 79, 80
Cheng, K., 78
China, 116, 133, 135, 142
Chinese students, 135, 136, 141, 142, 144
chocolate calculator, 159
Clark, H., 78
Coben, D., 58–9, 64, 157
cogs, 168
conceptual organisation, 138
Cooke, S., 146
Coupland, J., 170
Coxhead, A., 44
Crompton, K., 78
Croon, M., 96
Crowther, J., 14
cultural attitudes, 139–43
cultural capital, 1, 2, 5–7, 137
cultural differences, 134
Cultural Studies, 146

culture shock, 134, 139
  acculturation process, 143–5
  cultural attitudes towards education, 139–43
  foundation programme, implications for, 145–8
  language acquisition, 135–8
  language and conceptual organisation, 138
curriculum-based language support, 42
Cushner, K., 140

D
Data Driven Learning (DDL), 46
David, M., 27
de Oliveira, J. M., 96
Didion, J., 46
digital footprints, 130
digital literacy, 130
Dillabough, J., 3
discourse, 47–8, 53
diverse community, 148
Dodd, M., 59, 61
Donaldson, J. F., 14
Dornyei, Z., 97
Driving Force, 184
Duffin, J., 59, 63
Durham University Foundation Centre, 20, 28, 37, 38, 41–2, 48, 91, 96, 105–7, 119, 121, 124–5, 141, 152, 155
Durham University On-line (DUO), 147

E
EAP Toolkit, 49
Earth Science, 77, 80–81
Educational Maintenance Allowance (EMA), 11, 12
Edwards, J., 137

Effectively Maintained Inequality (EMI), 22
Egerton, M., 3
e-learning solutions
  preparedness, 76–8
  visualisation, 78–82
elite universities, 8–9
Elliot, A. J., 172
Elluminate, 126
emotional intelligence, 168, 175
emotional system, 165–6
emotions
  after class and, 171–2
  building resilience, 173–4
  in classroom, 171
  emotional system, 165–6
  pre-course preparation of students, 169–70
  preparing teaching materials, 170–1
  public performance, 168–9
  students and, 166–8
  tests and examinations, 172–3
Employability and Enterprise Centre, 129
Engineering courses, 32
English for Academic Purposes (EAP), 42, 45, 51
English universities, 20
Enhancing the Student Experience, 94
entry requirements, 36, 37, 41, 92
ethnic minorities, 3–4
European Union (EU) provision, 28–33
Evans, J., 60, 153, 154
exercise, 78, 81, 174

F
Facebook, 105–7
  challenges and opportunities, 114–16
  Foundation Centre on, 109–14
  investigating use, 107–9
  multi-channel future, 116
facilitating subjects, 7, 8
fair access, 95
Feak, C. B., 47
FE College. *See* Further education (FE) college
fees, effect of, 10–12
female students, 4
Ferrie, A., 26
field, 1–2
Figueras, O., 63
finance, effect of, 10–12
focus group, 135
Force Concept Inventory (FCI), 66, 68
formal methods, 63–5
former students, interviews with, 124–6
Foundation Centre, 28–30, 107, 119, 125, 126
  additional language support, 42–3
  audio feedback, 51–2
  cohort, 41–2
  curriculum-based language support, 42
  discourse, 47–8
  FOCUS corpus, 50
  glossary, 49
  grammar, 45–7
  lexis, 43–5
  mathematics, 57–8
  phonology, 48–9
  text inclusion, criteria for, 50–1
FOundation CorpUS (FOCUS), 44, 46, 50, 53
Foundation Family, 109
foundation programmes, 27–8
  feed forward, 187
  HE, alienation with dominant culture in, 185–7
  implications for, 145–8

inadequate initial education, 181–4
modelling, 36–7
motivations for developing, 35–6
recruitment bias, 184–5
UK, 27–8
foundation year provision, 19–20
  access to higher education diploma, 26–7
  foundation degrees, 27
  foundation programmes, 27–8
  home and European Union (EU) provision, 28–33
  international provision, 34–5
  modelling, different foundation programmes, 36–7
  motivations for developing foundation programmes, 35–6
  Open University, 24–6
  UK, foundation programmes in, 28
fragile achievers, 153, 157
free school meals (FSM), 6
Frijda, N. H., 175
Funder, D., 96
Further education (FE) college, 26, 29, 180
Further Education Institution (FEI), 23, 27
FutureLearn, 122

G
Gagné, R., 60
Gardner, Chris, 98
General Certificate of Education (GCE), 5, 27
General Certificate of Secondary Education (GCSE), 6, 32, 62, 152–3
geography, 81
geology, 81
Gilbert, J. K., 75
Gisbert, M., 96

glossary, 49
Golby, J., 96
Goldthorpe, J. H., 21
Gorard, S., 4, 5, 12, 13
Grade Point Average (GPA), 96
grammar, 45–7
Greenfield site, 59

H
habitus, 1–2, 10
Hake, R. R., 69
Hall, A. G., 14
hardiness, 96, 97
Hatherly, P. A., 76
Hayes, T. J., 107
Hayward, E. O., 170
Heidig, S., 170
Higgit, D. L., 77
higher education (HE), 19, 41, 179
  alienation with dominant culture in, 185–7
  capital, habitus and field, 1–2
  ethnic minorities, 3–4
  fees and finance, effect of, 10–12
  female students, 4
  habitus, effect of, 10
  low socioeconomic backgrounds, students, 3
  mature students, 4
  for non-traditional students, 95
  reproduction of society; elite universities, admissions bias in, 8–9; France, selection in, 7; UK, selection in, 7–8
  under-representation, 12–13; A-level system, 6–7; cultural capital and inadequate compulsory education, 5–6; rational decision/unconscious action, 14
  unfair under-representation, 4–5

Higher Education Academy (HEA), 120
higher education institutions (HEIs), 3, 4, 7, 13, 25, 120, 122
Hoare, A., 93–4
Hockings, C., 146
Holmberg, M., 79
Homer, B. D., 170
Hout, M., 22
Hyland, K., 43–4

I
image-based AR, 78
imposter syndrome, 186
inadequate compulsory education, 5–6, 179, 181–4
independent learning, 130
informal methods, 62–5
information technology (IT) blackboard systems, 159
initiatives, 23–4
institutional denigration, 161
interactive screen experiments (ISEs), 76, 82–5, 124
International English Language Testing System (IELTS), 41, 48, 49, 135
International Foundation Year qualification, 42
International Phonetic Alphabet (IPA), 48–9
international provision, 34–5
international students, 34, 42, 47–9, 52, 73, 83, 123, 135, 137, 141, 145, 147

J
Johnstone, A., 45, 75, 76
Johnston, R., 93–4
Jordan, S. E., 76

K
Karsenty, R., 59, 152
Keenan, C., 120, 122
Kim, Y. Y., 144
Kind, P. M., 74
Kirstein, J., 76
Klinger, C., 152
knowledge economy, 90
Knowles, M., 57–9

L
Lack of Regulation, 96
Lai, A., 141
laissez-faire approach, 109, 110
Land, R., 67
language, 138
 additional language support, 42–3
 audio feedback, 51–2
 curriculum-based language support, 42
 discourse, 47–8
 FOCUS corpus, 50
 Foundation Centre cohort, 41–2
 glossary, 49
 grammar, 45–7
 lexis, 43–5
 phonology, 48–9
 text inclusion, criteria for, 50–1
language acquisition, 135–8
Language Lunches, 42, 45
language support initiatives, 49
Lannin, J., 155
Lantolf, J. P., 138
Larsen, R. J., 175
Laurillard, D., 52, 83, 84
Laws, D., 92
Leopold, J., 26
lexis, 43–5
lifelong learning, 12, 13, 29
Linnenbrink-Garcia, L., 166
Litherland, K., 82

Lithner, 64
live webchats, 126
location-based Augmented Reality, 78
lower socioeconomic group (LSE), 90, 91
Lucas, S. R., 21, 22
Luckmann, T., 10, 137, 144
Lüdtke, O., 95
Lumsden, E., 121, 122

M
Maier, M. A., 172
Marshall, C. A., 96
Marton, F., 99
massive open online courses (MOOCs), 122
mathematics
  affective issues, 151–4
  avoiding labels and self- or institutional denigration, 161
  belief and attitude, 154–6
  constructive student–student and student–tutor interactions, 157–9
  Foundation Centre cohort, 57–8
  graduated exposure, 159–61
  improve students' Newtonian way of thinking, 67–8
  making common issues explicit, 156–7
  mental mathematics, 62–5
  misconception, 66–7
  self-directed learners, engaging with foundation students, 58–61
  success, measures of, 68–9
  teaching mechanics, 65–6
Matt, 180
Mattson, E., 106

mature students, 4, 11, 57
  admissions process, 91–5
  certain assets, 100
  driving force, 100
  fair access, 95
  method, 99
  non-traditional student, higher education for, 95
  personal qualities, 95–8
  phenomenography, 98–9
  toolkit, 100–1
  widening participation and importance of, 89–91
Maximally Maintained Inequality (MMI), 22
Mcbryde-Wilding, H., 121
Mcclain, T. M., 174
McClosky, J., 78
Mcdowell, A., 167
media, 84–5
mental mathematics, 58, 62–5
Meyer, J. H., 67
Microsoft Excel, 112
Milburn, Alan, 89, 91
Milburn Report, 24
Million+, 28, 29
Milson, C., 77
Minister of State for Universities and Science, 19
misconception, 65–7
moods, 175n1
Mori, S. C., 123
motivation, 97
Murphy, P., 136
music, 174

N
Nathan, P., 48
National Admissions Test for Law (LNAT), 92–3
National Scholarship Programme, 11, 19

National Statistics Socio-Economic Classification (NS-SEC), 3
National Student Survey, 51
Nation, I. S. P., 43
Neelsen, J. P., 21
negative self-image, 154, 156, 157
Netherlands, 96
network effect, 106
Newman, J. R., 174
Newson, C., 167
Newton, D. P., 99
Newtonian mechanics, 58
Newton, L. D., 99
Newton's laws, 66–8
Niggli, A., 96
1994 group, 28, 33, 94
Noftle, E., 96
non-traditional students, 24, 90
 higher education for, 95
 international student
  acculturation to, 134;
  acculturation process, 143–5;
  cultural attitudes towards
  education, 139–43;
  foundation programme,
  implications for, 145–8;
  language acquisition, 135–8;
  language and conceptual
  organisation, 138
 language issues; additional
  language support, 42–3;
  audio feedback, 51–2; cohort,
  41–2; curriculum-based
  language support, 42;
  discourse, 47–8; FOCUS
  corpus, 50; Foundation Centre
  cohort, 41–2; glossary, 49;
  grammar, 45–7; lexis, 43–5;
  phonology, 48–9; text
  inclusion, criteria for, 50–1
Nordmeier, V., 76
North-East UK university, 96

O

Office for Fair Access (OFFA), 20, 37, 89
Ohm's law, 79
Old university, 22
one right method, 62–5
Open University, 11, 24–6
Osborne, J., 74
Osborne, M., 26
outreach activities, 20

P

Pascarella, E. T., 168
Passeron, J., 10
Patterns and Trends in UK Higher Education 2013, 34
Pekrun, R., 166, 172
personal qualities, 95–8
phenomenographic method, 99
phenomenography, 98–9
phonology, 48–9
photograph-based Flash software, 76
physics, 57, 75, 77, 78, 85
Pickford, R., 51
Plass, J. L., 170
positive reinforcement, 155
post-compulsory education system, 15
practical science
 implementation and analysis, 82
 preparedness, 76–8
 preparing for, 74–5
 visualisation, 75, 78–82
pre-arrival provision, 122–3, 127–8
private education, 8
Project 2000, 185

Q

Quality Assurance Agency (QAA), 73

R
Race, P., 51
Raftery, A. E., 22
Ramsden, P., 52
rational decision, 14
Reay, D., 3, 13
recruitment bias, 184–5
relaxation, 174
repair theory, 155
Reproduction in Education, Society and Culture, 10
retention rates, 24, 26–8
Rethinking University Education, 83
Richardson, J., 26
Robbins, D., 2
Roberts, B., 95
Robins, R., 96
Rose, H., 121
Rubenson,K., 14
Ruschman, D., 107
Russell Group, 8, 9, 31–3

S
Saunders, M., 167
Schmitt, D., 44
Schmitt, N., 44
Schnyder, I., 96
Schoenfeld, A., 58, 59, 64
Schumacher, D., 76
Schwartz Report, 94
Scottish Access courses, 29–31
self denigration, 161
self-directed learners, 58–61
self-efficacy, 97–8, 154, 155, 172
Selwyn, N., 12, 13
Sheard, M., 96
Simpson, A., 59, 63
Sixth Form college, 23
Sixth Form colleges, 29
social capital, 1, 2
social inequality, 21

social interaction, 174
socialisation, 143
socialisation process, 10
social media, 105–7
social mobility, 1, 3, 13, 15, 21, 90, 184
Sowton, C., 47–8
Standard English (SE), 46
state education, 8
Stott, T., 78, 80, 82
structural locus of delivery, 36–7
student-centred pre-arrival platform, 124–6
student engagement, 127–8
Student Room, 116
student–student interactions, 157–9
Student Success and National Research Center on Education, 98
student–tutor interactions, 157–9
Supporting Professionalism in Admissions (SPA), 92, 93
Sutton Trust, 8, 23–4
Swales, J. M., 47

T
Talanquer, V., 75
Taster Day, 157
teaching practices
 after class, 171–2
 building resilience, 173–4
 in classroom, 171
 emotional system, 165–6
 pre-course preparation of students, 169–70
 preparing teaching materials, 170–1
 public performance, 168–9
 students and, 166–8
 tests and examinations, 172–3

technical vocabulary, 43
Terenzini, P. T., 168
text inclusion, 50–1
Thayer, R. E., 174
Theyssen, H., 76
Thomas, L., 120, 121
threshold concepts, 65–6
Tight, M., 5, 90
Tobias, 151
Townsend, B., 155
Trautwein, U., 95
Treagust, D. F., 75
Treiman, D. J., 21
Trimble, L., 44
Tsai, C.-C., 78
Tse, P., 43–4
Tutorial-Simulations, 84

U

UK
 foundation programmes in, 28
 selection in, 7–8
 university, 142; challenges and opportunities, 114–16; Foundation Centre on Facebook, 109–14; investigating Facebook use, 107–9; multi-channel future, 116; social media and recruitment, 105–7
UK Clinical Aptitude Test (UKCAT), 93
Um, E., 170
unconscious action, 14
Universities and Colleges Admissions Service (UCAS), 32, 33, 91–5
University Alliance, 28
University and Colleges Admissions Services (UCAS), 8, 9
University Challenge report, 91

university life
 critical phase, 120–2
 distance, supporting students at, 128–9
 key findings and future work, 129–1330
 pre-arrival portal impact, evaluating, 127–8
 pre-arrival provision, 122–3
 student-centred pre-arrival platform, 124–6
University of Stirling, 26
University of York, 122

V

Van Bragt, C., 96
Vermunt, J., 97
virtual field trips, 78, 81, 85
virtual learning environment (VLE), 109, 124
visualisation, 75, 78–82
vocabulary, 43–15, 47, 146, 169

W

Wagerman, S., 96
Walker, M. M., 107
Waller, R., 123
Warburton, J.77
Western universities, 133, 147
widening participation (WP), 11, 15, 19, 20, 89–91, 93
 access to higher education diploma, 26–7
 foundation degrees, 27
 foundation programmes, 27–8
 Open University, 24–6
 Sutton Trust, 23–4
 widening provision lead, 21–2
Williams, S., 160
Woodley, A., 24

Y

Yorke, M., 3, 121
Young, P., 167

Z

zone of comfort, 147
Zinck Stagno, M., 107

Printed by Books on Demand, Germany